Campagnolo

PAOLO FACCHINETTI
GUIDO P. RUBINO

75 years of cycling passion

Opposite the title
Fausto Coppi in the rainbow jersey of the world champion studies the mechanics of his bicycle.

page 6
The cyclist Tullio Campagnolo at the pass of Croce d'Aune, November 1927.

Velo Press
1830 North 55th Street
Boulder, Colorado 80301-2700 USA
303/440-0601 • Fax 303/444-6788
E-mail velopress@insideinc.com

Editorial coordination: Gino Cervi

Paolo Facchinetti wrote all the chapters of this book except *Inside the factory*, which is an elaboration by Gino Cervi of interviews performed at Campagnolo in February 2008. Guido P. Rubino wrote and edited all the information on Campagnolo products, the *Brief history of the gear changer* (page 152), *Campagnolo instructions for use: 10 practical suggestions* (page 155), and provided consultation on all the technical subjects presented in the book.

Editorial direction: Elisabetta Longhi

Editing: Gino Cervi, Antonio Gurrado

Picture research: Giovanna Bertelli

Design and layout: Break Point

Photolithography: Serio s.p.a., San Paolo d'Argon, Bergamo

Original title: *Campagnolo: La Storia che ha cambiato la bicicletta*
First published in Italy in 2008 by Bolis Edizioni s.r.l., Azzano San Paolo (BG), Italy
Copyright © Bolis Edizioni s.r.l., Azzano San Paolo (BG), Italy
English translation copyright © Bolis Edizioni s.r.l., Italy
All rights reserved. www.bolisedizioni.it

English translation: Jay Hyams

Composition: Michael Shaw

Translation, editing, and composition coordinated by LibriSource, Inc.

The text of this book is composed in Scala Sans Light with the display set in Caxton Book.

All rights reserved
Printed in China
First English-language edition

Distributed in the United States and Canada by Publishers Group West.

Library of Congress Cataloging-in-Publication Data
Facchinetti, Paolo.
 [Campagnolo. English]
 Campagnolo : 75 years / Paolo Facchinetti and Guido Rubino.
  p. cm.
 Includes bibliographical references and index.
 ISBN 978-1-934030-37-0 (pbk. : alk. paper)
1. Campagnolo S.r.l.–History. 2. Bicycles–Italy–Parts–History.
3. Campagnolo, Tullio, 1901-1983. 4. Bicycle industry–History.
I. Rubino,
Guido. II. Title.
 TL437.5.C36F33 2008
 629.227'20945–dc22

                              2008022798

No part of this book may be reproduced, stored in a retrieval system or transmitted, in any form or by any means, electronic or photocopy or otherwise, without the prior written permission of the publisher, except in the case of brief quotations embodied in critical articles and reviews.

For information on purchasing VeloPress books, please call 800/234-8356 or visit www.velopress.com

08 09 10 11 / 10 9 8 7 6 5 4 3 2 1

Special thanks to
Valentino Campagnolo, president and general director of Campagnolo s.r.l. , for permission to consult the Campagnolo archives; Lorenzo Taxis, director of marketing and communications of Campagnolo s.r.l., for his support for the editorial project; Francesco Zenere, director of public relations of Campagnolo srl, for his assistance in creating the book; Gianni Borga, Gabriele Ciavatta, Giuseppe Dal Prà and Valentino Franch for their participation in interviews; Marcello Capobianchi and Fulvio Lo Monaco for making pieces from their collections available to be photographed; and Lauretta Binda, Antonio Colombo, Cicli de Rosa, Paolo Gandolfi, Giuseppe Genazzini, Alberto Masi, Sabrina Sandri.

Contents

Campagnolo - Tullio

The legend of Croce d'Aune

It was a cold and rainy day, that November 11, 1927. In the Veneto region of northern Italy they were racing the Gran Premio della Vittoria. Tullio Campagnolo, 27 years old, a racer from Vicenza with a passion for bicycle mechanics, had entered the race as an independent. Also in the race were some of the leading champions of the period: Domenico Piemontesi, Raffaele Di Paco, Federico Gay. The moment came that Tullio found himself sprinting alongside those three famous men. All four of them, moving fast, were climbing the twists and turns of the road that leads from Feltre to Croce d'Aune, a pass at the altitude of 1,020 meters, on the Sovramonte plateau in the Alpi Bellunesi. Tullio felt good, good enough to imagine himself winning the race. But the weather was getting worse, the rain had turned into snow, and the ascents were getting harder and harder. It was time to change gears.

In those days, changing gears meant stopping, getting off the bike, removing the rear wheel, then spinning it around to insert the chain on a different sprocket on the other side of the hub, one that would make pedaling easier. Tullio got off and set to work removing the wheel. But his hands were nearly frozen, and he couldn't get a firm grip on the wingnuts. Only after several endless and anguished seconds, with his fingers bleeding from the effort, did Tullio succeed in releasing and removing the wheel. But his dream of victory had vanished with his three companions in the sprint, by then climbing a hill far from where he stood. Between one curse and another, it was in that moment and at that place that, according to legend, Tullio Campagnolo spoke the phrase that was to change his life and also the entire history of modern cycling. Speaking in his Vicenza dialect, he said, *"Bisogna cambià qualcossa de drio"* ("Something in the rear must change"). It was true. It was high time someone brought the rear wheel of a bicycle into the modern age.

Campagnolo finished fourth, and angry. But as of that day his mechanical genius had another, more important finish line to reach. He wanted to find a way to more easily release the rear hub as well as a way to change gears without having to get off the bicycle, without having to lose precious time. He achieved his goal in three years, registering a trademark for his "quick-release hub," technically defined as "gearing for cycling."

It was the beginning of a long story—a story that was to make Campagnolo not only a name but a symbol, a symbol of the most advanced mechanical technology applied to the bicycle.

The history of cycling can be divided into two great periods: B.C. (Before Campagnolo) and A.C. (After Campagnolo). The B.C. period was a dark age in which racers faced nearly inhuman conditions, riding iron velocipedes over outrageously poor dirt roads. Then came the dawn of the A.C. period, a time in which the enlightened genius of one man found the way to alleviate the suffering of cyclists by perfecting the gear changer (sometimes improperly called the "speed changer"). As has been written elsewhere, Tullio Campagnolo introduced "the bicycle motor" to cycling.

For a long time, the idea of a gear changer met stiff opposition from purists and poets of bikes races, such as Henri Desgrange, founder of the Tour de France. Desgrange believed that a racer had to confront all difficulties and asperities using nothing more than his own personal strength, without any human or mechanical assistance. But even the famed patron of the Tour, the man who sang of the "magnificent brutality of the races," was forced to give in to reality, since the ingenious novelty of the "changer" was an absolute necessity if racers were to make it over the Alps and the Pyrenees.

So it came to be that a certain locality, the pass of Croce d'Aune, entered the history of cycling. In June 1995, in memory of the moment in which young Tullio was struck by the flash of inspiration for his revolutionary invention, a monument was set up on the site honoring him and also his legend. For indeed Campagnolo has become truly legendary within the world of cycling. Many companies have competed with Campagnolo, and many continue in that competition. But just as the name Ferrari stands for race cars, Rolls-Royce for luxury cars, and Armani for elegance in dress, Campagnolo is, by definition, the component maker for bicycles.

What follows is the history of a man and a company destined to always be part of the history and culture of sport.

The Origins of the Bicycle:
Mechanics, Artisans, Industry

1816: an idea
born of a volcano

Bicyclemania: races,
pioneers, heroes

Gentlemen, change
your gears!

Invented after the locomotive and before the automobile, the bicycle is one of the machines emblematic of the technological progress of the 19th and 20th centuries. The bicycle is "the marvelous instrument to which, it must be admitted, we owe all the movement that, in less than half a century, transformed all of modern society and led from the velocipede all the way to the airplane" (M. Violette, Le Cyclisme, Paris, 1912).

1816: an idea born of a volcano

Before entering the heart of our story, let us quickly review the genesis and evolution of the bicycle.

The idea for the bicycle became solid reality in 1816. The year before, the Tambora volcano in Indonesia had erupted, an explosion so massive and prolonged that within a few months the quantity of volcanic ash in the atmosphere had caused global climatic changes, lowering temperatures by as much as 5° F. (3° C.). The volcanic material absorbed so much solar radiation that in North America and northern Europe 1816 became known as "the year without a summer." Spring frosts damaged crops; New England had blizzards in July. The lack of fodder killed off a dramatic number of horses, at the time the most important means of transportation (George Stephenson's locomotive was still a few years in the future). The German baron Karl Drais von Sauerbronn of Mannheim, grandson of the grand duke of

The bicycle

Made of metal, early bicycles were lighter than the preceding velocipedes. The disproportionate size of the front wheel increased the distance covered by a single turn of the pedals, but keeping the bicycle upright and not running over pedestrians required a certain skill . . .

Baden, was a kind of amateur inventor: his fervid imagination had already led to several inventions, including a vehicle for traveling underwater, a periscope, and a typewriter. In 1813 he had presented a four-wheeled car to Czar Alexander, then visiting Baden. In that dramatic 1816 he sought to find a replacement for the horse. Not too many years earlier, in 1791, another noble, the French count Mede de Sivrac, for his own amusement, had connected two wheels with a bar that he could sit on and thus push himself along with his feet, much to the amused delight of his subjects. A small detail: Sivrac's *celerifere*, as it was called, had no steering device, so unless the road ahead ran straight the count always ended up in a ditch. It must be said that recent research into this story has revealed that Sivrac's invention may instead be nothing more than a fabrication put together by a French journalist who, in the period of anti-German sentiment following the French defeat at Sedan in 1870, tried with this story to establish French primacy over the detested Germans at least in terms of the paternity of the bicycle.

Indeed, many men and even entire civilizations contend for paternity of the bicycle. From time to time historians identify the bicycle's beginnings among the Sumerians, the Etruscans, and as with everything else, the Chinese. Some see Leonardo da Vinci as the bike's true father: in the Codex Atlanticus (Vol. II, folios 132–33) there is the sketch of a bicycle fitted with a chain drive, but by now it seems confirmed that this childish charcoal sketch was made by a workshop assistant, although it may be a copy of an original design by Da Vinci himself (there is a known Leonardo drawing of a chain with cube-shaped teeth in the Codex of Madrid).

Drais's vehicle did not come to much. His wooden two-wheeled velocipede was pushed along with the feet and was equipped with both a handlebar and a saddle. In time of need, it could certainly have taken the place of a horse to cover certain distances, hence the boast that it "saved

Bicycle or horse?

A calendar from 1894 from
La Rivista Velocipedistica. In
these years, the bicycle was
presented as an alternative
to the horse. It was not rare
for races to be held between
the two means of locomotion
to see which would prove
the faster.

feed." The baron patented his invention in 1817 and began selling it. He called it the *Laufmaschine* ("running machine"), although it is best known as the *draisine* and was nicknamed the dandyhorse. It did not meet with great success; even worse, Drais, who despite his noble origins was a fervid supporter of democratic ideas, found himself in trouble during that period of monarch restoration and ended up exiled to Brazil. He was back in Europe after only a few years but in that short time his invention had become outdated, completely surpassed by the rise of the locomotive. Drais died in poverty in 1851.

Of course the effects of the "year of the volcano" faded, horses once again prospered, and the "iron horse" began chugging into its heyday. All things considered, no one wanted to think about climbing onto heavy, unsteady, brakeless vehicles. Several decades had to pass before two-wheeled locomotion again intrigued the minds of inventors and mechanics. The second half of the 19th century was the age of positivism and faith in the progress of knowledge, science, and, most of all, technology. As the Italian philosopher and historian Benedetto Croce wrote of European society of that period: "Concern for things moral and political had diminished, but in its place had arisen a new fervor that was expressed in the tireless activity of industrial and commercial enterprises, technical discoveries, increasingly powerful machines, geographic exploration, colonization, and economic exploitation; in the tendency to give supremacy to scientific and practical studies; in the introducing and spreading of recreational activities and social games, to what is called sport, bicycles, and automobiles, boats and airships, boxing to football to skiing, all of which in various ways conspired to dedicate a great part of activities and interest to physical well being an physical skills . . . Many things were written against permitting running to become a passion, against the process of despiritualization, against letting sports destroy cultural ideals. The wind, however, was blowing in the opposite direction."

It was no easy life for the pioneers of cycling. The French newspaper *Le Gaulois* called cyclists "wheeled imbeciles." There was also the expression "bicycle face," meaning a face flattened by being crushed into the ground, a reference to what happened to those fearless fools who risked their

page 8
"Bicyclism"

Poster for a bicycle show
at the London Science
Museum in 1928. Made
by Austin Cooper.

Toulouse-Lautrec

Around 1896, William Spears Simpson, inventor of a patent for bicycle chains, commissioned French painter Henri de Toulouse-Lautrec to make an advertising poster for his product, the *chaîne Simpson*.

An English model

A Quad Stay by Eagle of 1899. By then the bicycle had assumed a structure destined to remain basically unchanged to today. It is the materials and the components that have changed.

lives on those terrible early bicycles. The Catholic curia prohibited priests from climbing aboard vehicles of that type, seen as a hardly dignified behavior; certain municipalities banned their circulation in populated areas, considering them dangerous to public safety; in most places women were vehemently prohibited from riding bikes, considered morally unseemly behavior because of the scandalous posture, not to mention the inevitable exhibition of ankles. Even so the spread of the bicycle seemed irresistible. The so-called "silent revolution" took the idea around the world, from France to England, Germany to the United States, Russia to Australia. The bicycle became the "steel horse."

Not too surprisingly, the first races, in the early 1870s, took place on race tracks for horses and often involved horses. Which of the two was faster? "It seems incredible"—this is from a newspaper of 1871, following a race with velocipedes—"that on somewhat bad roads one can ride a velocipede at speeds of one kilometer in three minutes, something that would be difficult to achieve even with a good horse."

Anyone, using nothing more than leg power, could set off the on the conquest of time and distance. Having established this basic truth, the effort was made to prove that bicycles were enormously reliable and strong. So it was that the early makers of bicycles, with the support of newspapers, began to organize long-distance races. The pioneering period of sport cycling had begun.

The year 1891 saw the Bordeaux–Paris of 572 km and the Paris–Brest–Paris of more than 1,200. The latter was won by the Frenchman Charles Terront in 71 hours; for three days and three nights he raced without stopping, demonstrating to the astonished public that the human body, if suitably trained, can survive astonishing demands and, perhaps most of all, that his 22-kilogram Humber bicycle, fitted with replaceable Michelin pneumatic tires, was able to overcome any obstacle. From that moment on Terront became "Napoterront," a nickname that elevated him to the rank of national hero.

Dates in bicycle history

1791 Count de Sivrac invents his *celerifere*, in wood without steering.

1817 Baron Karl von Drais constructs the *draisine*, in wood with steering.

1838 Kirkpatrick MacMillan, Scottish blacksmith, applies two foot rests to the front wheel. These keep the feet off the ground, thus also sparing shoes from the dirt.

1855 Ernst Michaux invents a system of bicycle traction powered by pedals fixed to a large front wheel.

1860 The wooden wheels of the bicycle are covered in iron, and the resulting vehicle is called a boneshaker, for obvious reasons.

1860 The first headlamps are fixed to bicycles, using candles or oil, for night riding. Also the first pairs of brakes are fitted.

1865 Arrival of the first frames made of hollow metal tubes and tires over wooden wheels; bikes come to weigh as much as 40 kg.

1866 The bicycle arrives in the United States thanks to Pierre Lallement, a former collaborator of Michaux who emigrated when his merits were not properly recognized. Together with James Carrol he obtains the first American patent for a bicycle.

1868 The Parisian watchmaker Giulmet has the mechanic Eugene Meyer build a velocipede with a chain drive on the rear wheel and, a year later, wheels with spokes.

1869 Jules Suriray adds ball bearings to wheel hubs.

1874 John Kemp Starley introduces the wheel with tangential steel spokes, giving bicycles increased stability and strength, and also builds the first bicycle made expressly for women, with a side seat and single pedal.

1878 Rousseau introduces the bicycle chain driven by the front wheel and, later, the rear wheel.

1888 James Boyd Dunlop of Scotland invents pneumatic tires with air chambers inside vulcanized rubber around the wheels.

1890 A sprocket is added to the rear wheel to make it possible to change the ratio of pedaling according to whether the road is flat or in ascent.

1891 The Michelin brothers invent replaceable tires.

1895 Jean Loubeyre invents the *polycelere* ("multispeed"), the first true derailleur, which will be advertised in the 1896 catalog of the Compagnie Generale des Cycles.

1897 The freewheel is introduced.

As the popularity of bicycles grew so did the manufacture of bicycles. Against the panorama of industrialization that, having begun in Great Britain, was rapidly expanding across Europe, the special sector devoted to bicycles and their components began to take shape and flower.

Famous men of the age, artists and writers, fell in love with the bicycle. Alexandre Dumas and Jules Verne; Gustave Dorè and Claude Debussy; Maurice Leblanc, creator of the character Arsène Lupin, and Victor Hugo.

Toulouse-Lautrec agreed to design the advertising poster for the Simpson bicycle chain (*La Chaîne Simpson*). Emilio Salgari paid homage to the new steel machine by writing a novel about it in 1895: *To the South Pole by Velocipede*. In 1899, right at the end of the decade, Pierre Giffard, director of the daily *Le Velo*, presented "La fin du cheval," an essay in which he claimed that "the end of the horse" had arrived, replaced in all respects by the bicycle.

Two years later, in 1901, Tullio Campagnolo was born.

From the horse to two wheels

An illustration presents the evolution from the 1700s to the 1800s of the first "pedaling machines."

Bicyclemania: races, pioneers, heroes

By the end of the 1800s the bicycle looked more or less like today's bicycles and was becoming one of the lead players in a period full of wonders on the threshold of enormous changes. The Wright brothers were trying to get an airplane to fly, Guglielmo Marconi was figuring out how to move words from one place to another, and Jules Verne lifted his characters off this planet and transported them all the way to the moon. Businessmen and adventurers experienced the pleasures of the Orient Express from Paris to Constantinople, while the automobile was steadily becoming the most revolutionary invention of a new century completely dedicated to movement and speed.

Of course, all these novelties were restricted to the lucky few. Ordinary people—the ones making up the overwhelming majority—dreamed of expanding their horizon by way of a bicycle. In 1894 the Touring Club Ciclistico Italiano came into being in Italy, an association that, by way of the bicycle—a bicycle wheel being the club's symbol—promoted a new geographical and territorial culture at the national level. Artisans were discovering how the two-wheeled vehicle could serve their profession: a knife grinder in Padua got rich by abandoning the aging donkey that had pulled his cart and using instead, even for trips to far places, a bicycle to which he had attached a grinding wheel.

1 L. Trousselier.
2 G. Garrigou.
3 Duboc.
4 L. Heusghem.
5 Blaise.

6 Ernest Paul.
7 J. Alavoine.
8 Masselis.
9 Godivier.

MAURICE GARIN
Vainqueur de la course Paris-Brest

L'Alcyon and Garin

For many years the French bicycle maker L'Alcyon sponsored a racing team. This ad from about 1910 shows some of the champions of the period: Louis Trousselier, Gustave Garrigou—winner of the Tour in 1911—and Jean Alavoine. Maurice Garin, winner of the first Tour, in 1903, is shown on the cover of *Le Petit Journal* while crossing the finish line in the Paris–Brest–Paris of 1901.

Bicycle races, including the big stage races, had proven the toughness of this machine, even when put to the harshest trials. The Tour de France (first run in 1903) and the Giro d'Italia (1909), carried out in sunshine or pouring rain, in mud or choking dust, on roads studded with holes or, at their very best, uneven, had turned out to be phenomenal testing grounds for bikes. Over periods of several consecutive days, the racers had to cover long distances that were not so much stages as journeys. They carried the necessary extra tires themselves along with bags loaded with food, changes of clothes, tools to repair brakes, bandages, and cures for fatigue that ran from wine flasks to chemical stimulants in tablet form.

The cyclists of the early 20th century performed the roles of pioneers, sometimes also of missionaries. They traveled across the land, visiting new places while being followed by journalists who wrote about their marvelous deeds, thus awakening the imaginations of readers, who longed to experience such adventures themselves. Some of that missionary zeal was behind the creation of the Tour de France—its racers carried around the country the idea of the bicycle as a reliable tool for traveling and for gaining new experiences. In the past France had been traveled by the *"compagnons du Tour de France,"* artisan masters who went from city to city teaching crafts to the young. Bicycle racers now did much the same, spreading the word about this vehicle that was itself emblematic of modernity.

The specialized mechanical industry and the artisans associated with it were only too happy to support this growing passion for bicycles. Even automobile makers saw the bicycle as a way to spread their name: Peugeot in France, Opel in Germany, and Fiat in Italy made bikes. The British Rudge and Rover, French Humber and Clement, and the American Wood Brothers had been the first in the world to adopt assembly lines, turning out a variety of products, such as sewing machines and motorcycles. In Italy, Lux and Mastrellat in Turin were the first to do this, but the center of the new industrial production was Milan, where Olympia, Bianchi, Prinetti-Stucchi, Dei, and Frera all prospered. Not too much later the former bicycling champions themselves founded new bicycle-making companies that thus had the guarantee of their glorious names: in Italy Ganna, Gerbi, and Maino; in France, Lapize, Christophe, and Alavoine.

Today's bicycle fans may give a little less weight to a bike's name, but in the past brand names were an important guarantee. In France: Alcyon, La Française, Automoto, Liberator, Metéore, Louvet, Labor. In Italy: Atala, Globo, Gloria, Bianchi, Maino, Legnano. Also profiting from the spreading popularity of the bicycle were the manufacturers of pneumatic tires (Wolber and Continental, Hutchinson and Dunlop, Michelin and Pirelli) as well as the makers of other related products, such as clothing. It was a phenomenon in continuous expansion, although occasionally slowed by wars, periods of economic recession, and social changes. Italy's Touring Club had 784 members in 1894, the year it was founded; by 1925 this number had risen to 357,000. In 1898 a census of bicycles in Italy had counted 185,000; twelve

years later there were 600,000, while France had more than 1 million bicycles by the beginning of the 20th century. The bicycle was a means of transportation, a means of amusement, but also more. Armies created corps of troops riding special bicycles for use in postal service, as first-aid medics, as explorers, even as front-line soldiers. Ottavio Bottecchia, the first Italian to win the Tour de France, served in World War I in Italy's bike-riding Bersaglieri. The bicycle he rode had been fitted with a machine gun.

Bicycles and the Great War

An Italian Alpine soldier with a bicycle in a photo taken by the writer Ugo Ojetti in 1915 at Cortina d'Ampezzo. Bicycles served important functions, primarily in communications, on both the front lines and in rear areas during World War I.

Gentlemen, change your gears!

Direct experience, especially that of professional riders, has always been of decisive importance in modifications of the details of bicycles. As early as 1904, for example, the idea had arisen of creating some sort of device to hold a foot more securely to the pedal; in 1927 the leather toe-clip came into being. In 1919 the Belgian racer Firmin Lambot had been the first to eliminate the awkward leather food bags attached to the front of handlebars, which aside from everything else did little for the bike's aerodynamics; instead he made use of two flasks. In 1939 Renè Vietto had the idea of hooking the flask to the downtube of the frame in order to reach it more easily. It was also Vietto who had his bicycling shoes perforated to improve the airflow to his feet.

The multiplicity of uses that had been found for bicycles—tourism, sport, work—sharpened the ingenuity of those who used them and manufactured them. Many of these efforts shared the same goal: to diminish the effort of pedaling. Not all roads are flat, and in countries like Italy and France the roads were composed of a series of ups and downs, hills and also quite high mountains. Climbing a hill meant a great deal of effort, and something had to be done to ease the labors of the cyclist. In 1905 the writer and bicycle-tourist Paul de Vivie undertook a trip over the Alps and invented a new system of derailleur: he mounted a second sprocket on the rear-wheel hub, on the side opposite the original sprocket. This second sprocket had two or three teeth more so as to provide the motive force needed for pedaling on ascents. To change from one sprocket to the other the rider had to dismount, take the wheel off, and turn it so that the chain would run on the different sprocket.

As so often happens with good new ideas, others sought to perfect the concept, in pursuit of a machine that would change gears with less fuss. Claudius Bouillier, for example, made several different versions of derailleurs over the course of the years. His most famous adaptations were Le Chemineau ("the vagabond"), mass produced and commercialized by Johanny Pannel in 1911, and Le Cyclo, made by Albert Raymond in 1924.

Professional racers were not permitted to make use of such ingenious devices. The prevailing philosophy—and it prevailed until the 1930s—was that of Desgrange, patron of the Tour de France and director of the magazine L'Auto. He believed a sporting gesture had validity only if the athlete could count on nothing more than his own strength, without the intervention of any sort of mechanical contraption. As he himself wrote: "I still feel that variable gears are only for people over 45. Isn't it better to triumph by the strength of your muscles than by the artifice of a derailleur? We are getting soft . . . as for me, give me a fixed gear!"

In 1905 Desgrange had introduced the Alps to the route of the Tour. In 1910 he went ahead and added the Pyrenees. He had dispatched a representative, Alphonse Steines, to report on the conditions in those more or less uninhabited and inhospitable mountains. Steines spent many days struggling through the wild

1909: the first Giro

The first Giro d'Italia began in Milan on May 13, 1909. This commemorative postcard indicates the route taken and presents the leaders of the race, including, at the lower center, Luigi Ganna, the winner.

The strength of Maino

Maino of Alessandria was one of Italy's oldest bicycle manufacturers. This poster proclaims the brand's special strength in an eloquent way.

**The lightness
of Peugeot**

An ad from the 1930s for Peugeot bicycles. Like many other automobile manufacturers, Peugeot made bicycles, beginning its production at the end of the 1800s.

countryside, was forced to abandon his automobile and continue on foot, all the while encountering endless difficulties, but in the end he telegraphed his boss: "Very good road. Perfectly practicable." In truth, those mountain roads were disastrous mule tracks, traversed with difficulty even by mountain goats or cows on their way to pasture; the bicycle racers who were forced to pedal over them experienced a kind of living hell. Pushing his bike up the Col d'Aubisque in the Pyrenees, and on the brink of an hysterical breakdown, Octave Lapize—who

Tour de France Montée du Col d'Allos

ÉQUIPE
AUTOMOTO-HUTCHINSON
FREÍNS TOURISTE-BOWDEN

BOTTECCHIA
GAGNANT DES
TOURS DE FRANCE 1924&1925

**Bottecchia wins
the Tour**

Racing for the French
Automoto-Hutchinson team,
Ottavio Bottecchia was the
first Italian to win the Tour de
France, in 1924, a victory
repeated the next year.

went on to win that Tour de France—caught sight of Desgrange and screamed at him a phrase destined for Tour history: *"Vous êtes assassins!"* ("You're murderers!"). A look of sarcastic satisfaction is said to have crossed the face of the patron of the French race.

The racers in the Giro d'Italia of 1914, perhaps the most grueling of the so-called heroic age of cycling, also found themselves on their feet pushing their bikes. The first stage of that race, involving more than 400 kilometers, made them cross Sestriere (2,035 meters altitude). There were 81 of them when they set off, of whom 47 turned back. Gremo and Gann, Gerbi and Girardengo had to push their bikes for kilometer after kilometer climbing on foot through mud and snow.

During this heroic age, bicycle racers—in part because of the ordeals they had to face, which seemed like punishments—were looked upon as supermen. In 1924 Albert Londres, a famous correspondent for a Parisian daily, referred to them instead as "convicts of the road." He had just done a report on the forced labors of convicts in the penal colony of Cayenne in French Guiana. Sent to cover the Tour de France, he had found little difference between the inhuman conditions of the prisoners and those faced by the cyclists.

Quite clearly, this situation could not be permitted to continue forever, and it was not long before racers were given at least the opportunity to ease their pedaling by adding two or more sprockets to the rear hub so as to take on the steeper ascents with less fatigue. This was in part the result of pressure from the bicycle industry, which wanted to see official recognition given to the contributions made by specific bicycles in the glorious deeds performed by riders. Not all bicycles are equal, and a bicycle's strength and reliability were often of decisive importance.

There remained the fact that to change gears the rider had to get off his bike, release the rear wheel by twisting the wingnuts of the hub, spin the wheel around, then remount it, fitting the chain to the sprocket and then redoing the wingnuts. It was a complicated operation that often had to be performed under rain or snow or worse. And each time the result remained uncertain: it wasn't rare that after a few spins of the pedal the chain came loose.

So things stood in 1927, the year of Tullio Campagnolo's day in the snow at Croce d'Aune, the event that led to his quick-release hub, the first milestone in an authentic technological revolution.

Tullio, Homo Faber

Under the sign
of the file

The market,
the competition

The name, the brand:
communicating
Campagnolo

Everyone for Tullio,
Tullio for everyone

The unstoppable ascent of Tullio Campagnolo in the world of the racing bicycle took him from the workshop behind his father's hardware store, to his first patents, to the formation of Campagnolo s.r.l., to earning the respect and trust of the great champions of cycling. The ingenuity of his perceptions was a large part of his success, along with his tenacity in pursuing his goals, in promoting the brand and its products, and his energy and strategies as a great communicator. As Gianni Brera wrote, Tullio Campagnolo "for no less than half a century influenced and directed European cycling, from Di Paco to Magni, from Bartali to Coppi, from Adorni to Gimondi to Eddy Merckx."

Under the sign of the file

The young Tullio

In the 1920s Tullio
Campagnolo was a
promising cyclist.

The employee in the registry office in Vicenza considered himself a man of culture, or so it seems. When Valentino Campagnolo and Elisa Paiusco, reporting the birth of their second child, said they wanted to call him Tullio, the employee shook his head, scoffing at the ignorance of the poor, uneducated couple. In elegant handwriting he wrote in the register the name "Getullio," which—or so he had read in the *Italian Almanac* published by the Bemporad brothers—was derived from *Gaetullius*, meaning "originally from Gaeta," the sunny town south of Rome famous for its black olives. Little did it matter to the officious employee that coursing through the newborn's veins were several generations' worth of Veneto blood. When he was older, Getullio could not always disguise his displeasure at having to sign official documents with that bizarre name. Years later, however, he got even for the registry-office abuse by making the entire world learn to know him by his real name, the one his parents had wanted: Tullio Campagnolo.

On page 22
The first changer

Tullio Campagnolo and the
first dual-rod changer.

He was born August 26, 1901, in a house located between the hamlets of Ospitaletto and Anconetta on the eastern outskirts of Vicenza. In those early years of the 20th century, the Veneto was a land of poverty, and those were difficult times. Food was hard to come by. Many people had left or were planning to do so, as had throngs of people from the nearby regions of Piedmont, Emilia, and Friuli. People were dreaming of faraway lands, places where they might find hope for a better life, whether in the Americas or Australia.

The Campagnolos had chosen to stay despite the hardships. Elisa looked after the house and the two children and worked in the fields; Valentino got by with a small hardware store where he sold nails, screws, hooks, and whatever else his do-it-yourself neighbors might require. Connected to the small store was a true "workshop of miracles," a laboratory with tools and a blacksmith's worktable to forge shovels, sickles, harrows, wheels. So little Tullio grew up knowing something about his schoolbooks but a great deal

It began with a cart

The Campagnolo hardware store used a three-wheeled cart for the transportation of materials. Tullio built it himself.

The first advertisement

The first advertising notice for the Campagnolo gear changer on a page from the *Gazzetta dello Sport* in the 1930s.

Artisans and industry at Vicenza in the early 20th century

Early in the 20th century, Italy's Veneto was primarily an agricultural region, the major exception being the area around Vicenza, the region's only industrialized province. The entrepreneurial activity in that area had ancient historical and cultural roots. Indeed, the local population had always been involved in the making of

The Marzotto plant

The Marzotto Wool Mill in Valdagno is one of the oldest factories in the area of Vicenza. Founded in 1836, it converted to industrial activity in the early 1900s.

fabrics. By the opening years of the 20th century, the Lanificio Rossi in Schio, founded in 1817, was Italy's major wool manufacturer. During the 1920s the Marzotto wool mill at Valdagno, thanks to large investments in machinery and in the systematization of labor, rose to

international importance. In the early decades of the 20th century in the province of Vicenza the drive toward industrialization spread from the fabric sectors to other areas of production: tanning, papermaking, typography, gold working, and machinery (in 1911 there were 600 machinery shops in the area).

As industrialization slowly spread, the local industries were supported by a notable proliferation of artisan activity. The territory of Vicenza swarmed with small artisan workshops, most of them family-run. Many were the small shops like that of the Campagnolo family, places where the creativity and industry of individuals found expression. Even today, 24 percent of the working population in the territory of Vicenza is involved in the artisan sector.

In the 1930s many of these artisans continued to thrive in contrast to the serious economic recession that had hit Europe and Italy as a result of the American stock-market crash of 1929. Even so, by 1932 Italy was beginning to see a worrisome drop in production and exports, as well as a disturbing rise in unemployment. The state intervened the next year through the action of the Institute for Industrial Reconstruction (IRI), a public agency created to assist companies in crisis. Many artisans and small industries disappeared; the most courageous chose the route of "grow to not succumb," meaning they hoped to escape the crisis by making a leap ahead in terms of quality and size. For the most industrious, the old workshop with its cozy family intimacy was replaced by a noisy factory. So it was with Tullio Campagnolo.

more about files, pliers, anvils, vise grips, and hammers. He was fascinated by shaping and creating objects by folding metal as desired or as needed.

At 14, he attended the school of arts and crafts in Vicenza, studies that did not interfere with his completion of the practical part of his education in his father's workshop. At 18, he took part in a competition given by the railroad to become a machinist. The trains were wonderful

mechanical means, and at that time, 1919, in the first year after World War I, the railroad was expanding, having gone from being privately owned to state ownership. Tullio won the competition but was hired as a second machinist, a role that did not permit him to express his creativity in mechanical matters. He soon left the railroad and returned to work in his father's hardware store. There he could give free rein to his genius.

In the back room

Tullio Campagnolo at the work table in his father's old hardware store on Corso Padova, 101.

In the workshop of miracles, the young Campagnolo built his first bicycle, putting together and adapting scrap parts. He also built a three-wheeled van for his father to use when delivering new and repaired tools to clients. Standing out on the side, in white paint, was CAMPAGNO-LO FERRAMENTA with the address and telephone number. It seems that promoting the family company was a trait already developed in young Tullio's genes.

So fascinated was he by bicycles that he decided to become a racer. At that time, early in 1920, cycling was the most popular sport in Europe, and most of all in Italy. Newspapers used flowery prose when exalting the deeds of Costante Girardengo and Tano Balloni, Bartolomeo Aymo, Giovanni Brunero, and Ottavio Bottecchia, and news arrived from France and Belgium of the accomplishments of Henri Pelissier and Philippe Thjis, Jean Alavoine, and Gustave Garrigou.

At 21, wearing the jersey of the Veloce Club Vicentino, Campagnolo began racing. He was promising, well built and strong, and he found those who were willing to pay for him to pedal. First it was Cicli Aliprandi. Then Nicolò Biondo of Carpi paid his expenses and added something by way of incentive. Tullio took care of his bicycle with maniacal determination, always on the lookout for ways to improve its performance with small but ingenious improvements and adjustments, from the bottle holder to the brakes, from the crankset to the sprockets and the spokes.

Then came the day at Croce d'Aune. "I was paralyzed by the cold," he later recounted. "Working on the nuts, my hands began to bleed because the wheel would not come off. When I got home, defeated and discouraged, I began to think about what was to become the most perfect derailleur in the world."

The quick release

In the beginning was a nut that held the wheel fixed to the frame and the fork of the bicycle. Then technical evolution introduced the idea of gears to bicycles . . . and things changed.

Before the introduction of the derailleur, to move the chain it was necessary to remove, or at least loosen, the rear wheel. Having done so, the chain, no longer in tension, could easily be moved to the more appropriate gear on the rear hub. Once that operation had been performed, the wheel had to be put back in position and the nut had to be retightened.

This situation proved far less than practical. Operating a nut required use of a tool that was anything but easy to haul around on a bicycle. The change was thus made to wingnuts, nuts with the addition of extensions that made it possible to loosen them by hand. The practicality of wingnuts also proved limited. Road conditions in the days before asphalt meant the constant accumulation of dirt, not to mention the effects of dampness and oxidation, as well as freezing cold.

Such was the situation in which the cyclist Tullio Campagnolo found himself in 1927 on the road

Adjustment screws

The two screws at the sides of the cap opposite the quick-release lever make it possible to regulate the position of the hub axle and thus the amount of pressure applied when closing the quick release.

leading up to Croce d'Aune. Right there the idea began taking shape in his mind for the device that is at the heart of the Campagnolo patent that opened the way to a new age in bicycle mechanics: the quick release.

Tullio knew that screwing and unscrewing was not the most practical solution for a hub that must be rapidly manipulated. Far better would be a lever that released the hub without friction. The quick-release mechanism with its sliding skewer and eccentric made it possible to release the hub without friction. A second to open it, a second to close it. Changing gears became easier.

Although no longer necessary for changing gears, the quick-release mechanism has remained conceptually the same. When we see a racer quickly change a wheel, he is able to do so precisely because of that mechanism: the skewer inside a hollow axle with the easily operated lever. That same lever still bears the Campagnolo logo.

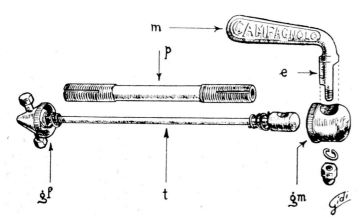

The quick-release mechanism

This diagram, taken from the March 1, 1950, issue of the magazine *Ciclismo Italiano*, shows that the quick-release mechanism is composed of a skewer inside a hollow axle. At one end of the skewer is a cone nut; at the other end is a quick-release lever fitted to an eccentric. Closing the lever makes the eccentric pull the skewer in, applying pressure that locks the hub to the rear dropouts of the frame or to the fork ends.

1930

Quick release

(Quick release: photo from a Campagnolo brochure without date) Picture of the first quick-release mechanism made by Campagnolo. Clearly visible is the threading at the ends of the hub that make it possible to mount a freewheel on one side and a fixed sprocket on the other.

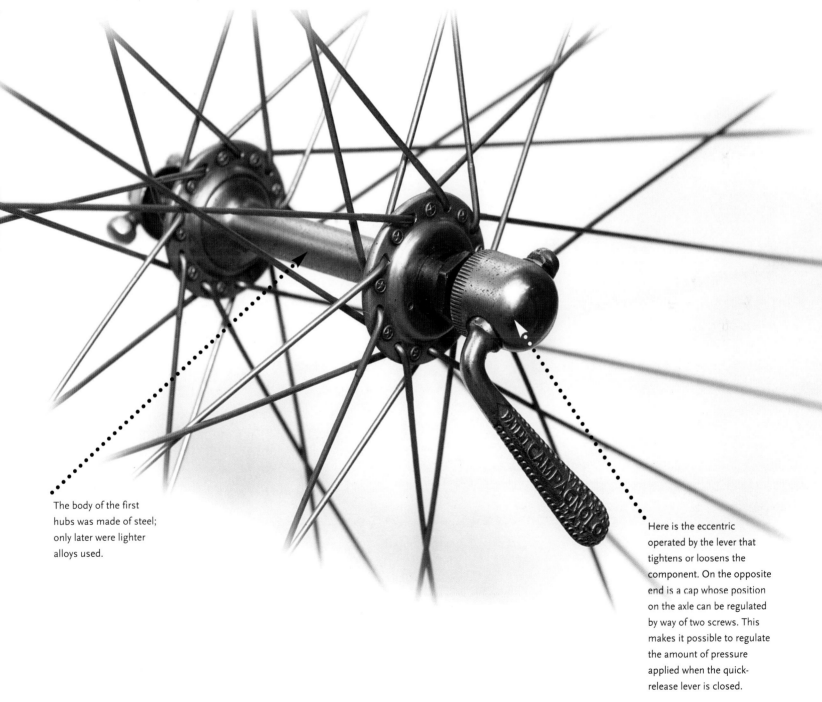

The body of the first hubs was made of steel; only later were lighter alloys used.

Here is the eccentric operated by the lever that tightens or loosens the component. On the opposite end is a cap whose position on the axle can be regulated by way of two screws. This makes it possible to regulate the amount of pressure applied when the quick-release lever is closed.

The market, the competition

It all began with that idea of releasing the rear wheel from its hub in a rapid and efficient way, using at least four fingers to operate a lever with wing nuts. On February 8, 1930, Tullio Campagnolo registered the first of his 185 patents, officially baptizing it "gearing for cycling." He had designed it at night on a sheet of paper and then had it made by the Fratelli Brivio of Brescia. He had tested it for a long time and now had to convince mechanics and racers to adopt it. At the same time he was already thinking of ways to further improve the device.

"Advertising is the soul of commerce," or so runs an old Italian adage. And Campagnolo, dynamic and ingenious, put it immediately into practice. Thanks to a loan of 3,000 lire from the lawyer Zilio Grande, he began to follow the races in every corner of Italy, showing everyone his quick-release hub and singing its praises.

When his "gearing for cycling" had won over enough converts—it was adopted by the leading bicycle producers Bianchi, Atala, Legnano, and Gloria—Tullio felt ready to take the big leap and go into mass production and commercialization. In 1933 he founded the Campagnolo company, with its headquarters in the back room of his father's workshop in Corso Padova, 101. Doing so took a good deal of courage. These were hard times financially, but also hard times for political reasons. Bicycle racers like Alfredo Binda and Learco Guerra were thrilling crowds with their astonishing feats, and future star Gino Bartali was beginning to make a name for himself, but Fascism took a stance that

The Nieddu brothers and the Vittoria Margherita

A four-page flyer of the times praised the qualities of the Cambio Vittoria Margherita and explained its function. The gear changer was defined (and one can sense a sort of comparative reference to the nascent Campagnolo changer) "the national gear changer par excellence, brought to the highest level of perfection by recent, very modern technical innovations to the chain self-derailleur, with which one can change gears while pedaling."

The flyer was also a kind of instruction manual, but the words illustrating its use involuntarily revealed its structural fragility:

1. Align the chain with the central cog of the freewheel.
2. Tighten the chain-guide-holder according to the width of the chain to avoid possible jamming between the tension roller and the chain-guide-holder.
3. The mechanical fingers of the self-derailleur, independent from one another, limit the movement of the chain among the various cogs of the freewheel; keep the chain from falling between the freewheel and the fork when changing speed; fix the self-derailleur in the position indicated in the drawing, tightening the screws to avoid rotation.
4. In changing gears, on flat ground or in ascent, continue to pedal to keep the upper extension of the chain at the correct tension.

was almost hostile to this sport. With its epic sense of brutal, physical exertion, cycling seemed closer to the peasant world than to the ideals of modernity, power, and speed that fed the regime's propaganda. "Cycling is in decline," newspapers announced in attempts to please the government. When in 1929 the weekly *Lo Sport Fascista* asked a variety of famous men to name their favorite sports, only two included cycling. Instead they praised other models of sporting activity, which were elevated to become emblems of Italian invincibility, from the Friulian giant Primo Carnera, champion of the world of heavyweight fighting in 1933, to the race car driver Tazio Nuvolari, victor at the wheel of roaring motorcars. There were also the middle-distance runner Luigi Beccali, gold medal winner in the 1,500-meter race in the Los Angeles Olympics in 1932, and the fencer Edoardo Mangiarotti, rising star of Italian fencing, destined to win a medal in Berlin four years later. Naturally the list included the national soccer players, the "Azzuri," world champions in 1934 and 1938 and winners at the Olympics in 1936. In 1934, twenty-five Italian athletes were summoned to present themselves at the Mostra della Rivoluzione Fascista to be decorated by Mussolini for sporting valor. Among them was not a single cyclist.

Obviously this attitude on the part of the ruling regime had a negative effect on the bicycle industry. Tullio Campagnolo was thus called upon to make hard sacrifices while continuing his work researching and perfecting bicycle technology while also doing the far-sighted work of promoting

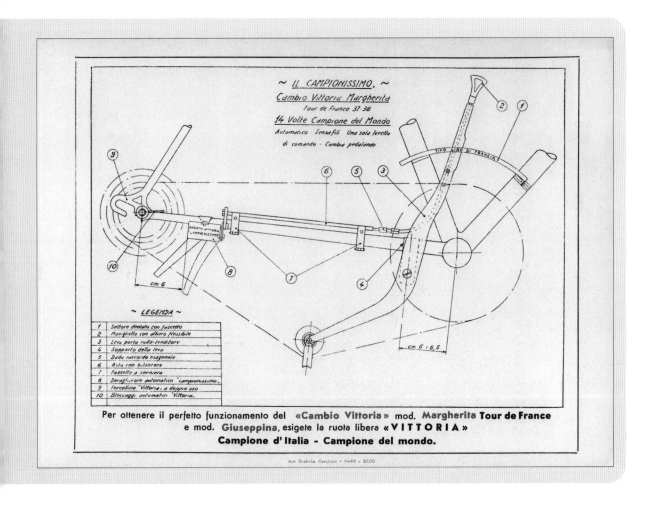

Di Paco in flight

Raffaele Di Paco, a Tuscan
sprinter who became a
professional racer in 1928,
was among the first to
believe in Campagnolo
products and to promote
them in the racing world.

himself and his activity. Traveling from race to race, Campagnolo talked to the professional cyclists and collected their ideas and suggestions. He reflected on all the information he gathered in the field, then picked up paper and pencil and drew designs, projects. He then took the next step, working with the tools in the back room of the hardware store. He created prototypes that served as production models, since he still entrusted the actual manufacture to others. The Fratelli Brivio company in Brescia guaranteed the quality that Tullio insisted on without a major outlay in terms of investing in materials.

But there was fierce competition in the field of parts for racing bicycles, both in Italy and overseas. A great many artisans were already busy working to resolve the problem of changing gears without having to dismount the bicycle. First among these were the brothers Amedeo and Tommaso Nieddu, Sardinian machinists who had moved to Turin and patented a complicated device that they guaranteed would offer great advantages to those who used it. Indeed, it assured its users nothing less than success, for which reason they called it the Vittoria ("victory"). This device consisted of a spring-loaded lever, with the chain-tightener ring

located at the far end of an extension arm reaching toward the ground and three gears mounted on the rear hub. It weighed 225 grams and was advertised as "an ingenious device; resistant to all stress, adaptable to any brand of bicycle, it has the enormous advantage of keeping the wheel constantly centered."

Ingenious, yes, but also devilishly complicated. To change gears, the racer had to make a sharp backpedal to block its action while at the same time reaching down to move the chain from one sprocket to the other with the fingers of one hand pressing on a lever fixed to the hub. Doing so often made the racer lose his balance or caused the chain to jam. Another problem was that the ring holding the chain extended to within inches of the ground, exposing the chain to dirt, dust, mud, rocks, and all the scraping and hitting caused by any unevenness of the road surface.

The Nieddu brothers immediately took stock of these problems and perfected their mechanism. A kind of shift stick was attached to the rear fork that made it possible to operate levers that moved the chain among four sprockets located on the same part of the wheel without having to use the fingers. This was baptized the Vittoria Margherita and

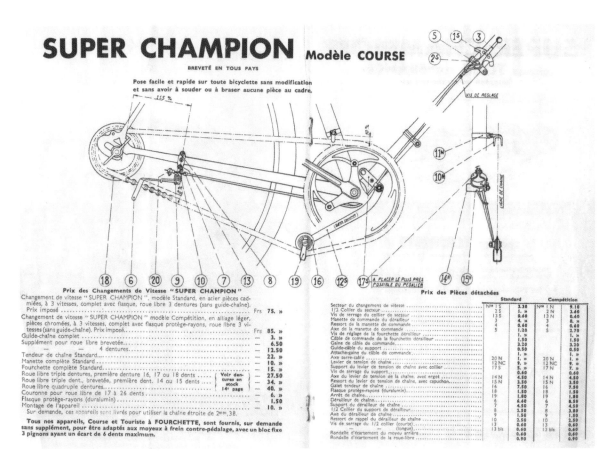

SUPER CHAMPION Modèle COURSE

BREVETÉ EN TOUS PAYS

Pose facile et rapide sur toute bicyclette sans modification
et sans avoir à souder ou à braser aucune pièce au cadre.

Prix des Changements de Vitesse "SUPER CHAMPION"

Changement de vitesse "SUPER CHAMPION", modèle Standard, en acier pièces cadmiées, à 3 vitesses, complet avec flasque, roue libre 3 dentures (sans guide-chaîne).
Prix imposé .... Frs 75. »
Changement de vitesse "SUPER CHAMPION" modèle Compétition, en alliage léger, pièces chromées, à 3 vitesses, complet avec flasque protège-rayons, roue libre 3 vitesses (sans guide-chaîne). Prix imposé............................... Frs 85. »
Guide-chaîne complet .... — 3. »
Supplément pour roue libre brevetée...................................... — 6.50
    —   —   4 dentures.......................... — 12.50
Tendeur de chaîne Standard... — 22. »
Manette complète Standard.. — 10. »
Fourchette complète Standard... — 15. »
Roue libre triple dentures, première denture 16, 17 ou 18 dents ..... — 27.50
Roue libre triple dent., brevetée, première dent. 14 ou 15 dents .... — 34. »
Roue libre quadruple dentures.. — 40. »
Couronne pour roue libre de 17 à 26 dents................................ — 6. »
Flasque protège-rayons (duralumin)....................................... — 1.50
Montage de l'appareil.. — 10. »

Sur demande, ces appareils sont livrés pour utiliser la chaîne étroite de 2mm,38.

Tous nos appareils, Course et Touriste à FOURCHETTE, sont fournis, sur demande sans supplément, pour être adaptés aux moyeux à frein contre-pédalage, avec un bloc fixe 3 pignons ayant un écart de 6 dents maximum.

The Super Champion

In 1937, Roger Lapébie of France won the Tour de France on a bicycle equipped with a Super Champion gear changer. This was a great publicity coup for the product, made by the Parisian Osgear company.

advertised—in the pompous Fascist style—as a product that exalted "Imperial Italy, vanguard of the world."

The Nieddu brothers also called the Vittoria Margherita "Il Campionissimo" ("the champion of champions") to emphasize its superiority over the competition. In 1935, Bartali was one of the first racers to use it, and, in 1938, when he won his first Tour de France, the five-sprocket model was baptized the "Giro di Francia." Later, during the 1940s, the Nieddu brothers made further improved versions of their device in duralumin (after the Margherita came the Cambio Giuseppina, also named for a daughter of the house of Savoy), diminishing its weight to only 100 grams.

During the postwar period, Tommaso Nieddu separated his activity from that of his brother and, together with Virginio Colombo and the Santamaria brothers, producers of the Fiorelli brand, at Novi Ligure, put new models on the market, such as the Cervino and the Stelvio, reworked versions of the French Super Champion. Using a Cervino, Alfio Ferrari won the amateur world championship in 1947 and Gino Bartali used it in 1949 on bikes built with his name by the Santamaria brothers. The fortune of the Vittoria and its derivatives came to an end in 1952 with the appearance of

other, more functional models, first among them those bearing the Campagnolo name.

During the 1930s, Tullio Campagnolo laid the basis for the success he achieved after the war. In so doing, he showed the wisdom of taking small steps. His objective, of course, was to connect the name of his product with that of a large industrial entity, such as the Legnano bicycle company with its champion racers Binda followed by Bartali, the Maino bicycles of Girardengo followed by Guerra, or of course the bicycles of Bianchi. But Tullio went about this slowly. First he sought approval and appreciation of his hubs and his gear changers from the bottom. The work required stubbornness and dedication. He went around to visit the mechanical workshops to show his pieces, which cost more than the others for the simple reason that Tullio refused to put up with ordinary materials and always wanted the best. This characteristic has remained a constant in the history of Campagnolo from the very beginning of the company to today.

Obstinate and insistent in his efforts to convince others, Tullio won the personal respect of both racers and mechanics. Among the first racers that Campagnolo could

The Simplex lever

Made by Simplex, this is one of the first front derailleurs. It worked in a very direct way, the cyclist operating a lever directly connected to the chain guide.

count on were his former racing friends. Among them was Raffaele Di Paco, born in Fauglia, just south of Pisa. A great sprinter and equally great lover, he was a genius and master of the unruly races of the 1930s. In 1935, Di Paco was the first to test the gear changer designed by Campagnolo and after using it convinced other cyclists to do likewise, among them Glauco Servadei, at Gloria, who won several stages in the Giro and the Tour between 1937 and 1940, and Primo Bergomi, a Genoese track cyclist, several times world record holder between 1939 and 1941. There was then the legendary encounter with Alfredo Binda, the nearly unchallenged dominator of Italian cycling from the mid-1920s until the opening years of the 1930s. He had just left racing, but his opinion was still of great importance in the world of cycling. The skeptical champion was given an improvised mechanical demonstration in the courtyard of his home at Cittiglio and promised he would do what he could to help Campagnolo spread word and use of his product.

Campagnolo knew what he had to do to enlarge his horizons. Between the end of the 1920s and the early 1930s, France had become a hotbed of highly equipped artisans taking on the search for the best system of changing the gears of racing bicycles. So in 1937 Tullio, despite the financial situation—his sister Amelia financed the trip—set off to follow the Tour de France, in part because for the first time in Tour history the organizers were permitting the use of gear changers. Gino Bartali was favored to win. He was riding a Legnano equipped with a Vittoria Margherita, but he was forced to withdraw from the race while wearing the yellow jersey—the famous *maillot jaune* that identifies the leader of the race—following a fall that occurred on the stage between Grenoble and Briançon. The winner was the Frenchman Roger Lapébie, riding a bike fitted with a Super Champion, and Campagnolo completed his international studies by getting a good look at the French competition.

1001 - CAMBIO CORSA CON MOZZI CALIBRATI **CAMPAGNOLO**

GINO BARTALI in piena azione sul Galibier durante il suo vittorioso Tour del 1948 con cambio **Campagnolo** corsa e mozzi calibrati con bloccaggi originali **Campagnolo**.

A RICHIESTA SI FORNISCONO I CAMBI CON LE MANIGLIE PIÙ LUNGHE PER CICLI DA TURISMO
NELLE ORDINAZIONI PRECISARE SE SI VUOLE IL DISCO PARARAGGI PER RUOTA LIBERA a 4 o a 5 PIGNONI

Bartali's winning gear shifter

From the Campagnolo catalog no. 12, published in 1953, a photo of Gino Bartali at the 1948 Tour de France, reaching for his dual-rod changer while ascending the Galibier pass. Bartali won that edition of the Tour.

The Super Champion and the Vittoria Margherita were the first gear changers authorized for use on the bicycles being used by racers in the Tour de France in 1937. The Super Champion, inspired by the Vittoria of the Nieddu brothers, had been made in Paris by the Swiss racer Oscar Egg and his Osgear company, in the early 1930s.

Egg, a former champion on roads and tracks of the years around World War I, held the world hour record three times between 1912 and 1914, won numerous six-day races (New York, Chicago, Ghent, and Paris), and won the 1914 Paris–Tours. He had raced for Griffon, Peugeot, and Bianchi, constantly increasing his mechanical knowledge. His gear changer had come into being in 1932 as the Champion; the next year it had evolved into the Super Champion, advertised as "the lightest and fastest." It had enjoyed immediate success, inspiring many additional models in the years to come. The victory in the 1937 Tour with Roger Lapébie was a great advertising coup for the Super Champion. Even so, the Osgear system had a decisive drawback. The chain stretcher, located beneath the chainwheel, was in an overly exposed position in terms of the many dangers on the road surface, and it was easy for a stone, or any obstacle, to bang into it, compromising its functioning. As with the Vittoria gear changer, the postwar Super Champion—despite victory in the World Road Racing Championships of 1946, with Hans Knecht—proved unable to evolve and keep up with the competition, and its fortune rapidly declined.

Constant Huret had also been among the top long-distance racers at the close of the 19th century: winner of the Bordeaux–Paris (594 km) of 1899, world record holder in the 6, 12, and 24 hours, he had been nicknamed "Le Grand

Constant" or even "The Baker," since that had been his trade before becoming a racing cyclist. Toulouse-Lautrec had used him as his model when he made the famous poster for Simpson chains. At age 35, Huret ended his racing career and, being passionate about bicycle mechanics, he later went into business with his two sons and set up a workshop in which he made sprockets and other bicycle parts. His first derailleur, the Criterium, enjoyed a certain amount of success, at first thanks to the accomplishments of the French racer (of Italian origin) Fermo Camellini, winner of the Flèche Wallonne in 1948, and later, most of all in the 1950s, thanks to the triumphs of Louison Bobet, victorious for three consecutive years in the Tour, from 1953 to 1955. The mechanism in the Huret gear changer was solid and robust but also heavy, so it was soon replaced by other systems. In the 1960s, the Jubilèe model, lighter and of the parallelogram type, permitted the brand to win back a certain degree of popularity. Acquired by Sachs in 1980, in 1997 Huret was incorporated into SRAM of the United States, which today is a competitor of both Campagnolo and Shimano.

But the true rival for the Campagnolo gear changer in the golden years of cycling, meaning the immediate postwar years, was the Simplex. Patented in the 1930s by the mechanic Lucien Juy of Dijon, it quickly rose to market dominance, with large-scale mass production. In 1933 alone, 40,000 examples were produced. Using a Simplex, the French champion Antonin Magne won the world road-racing title at Bern in 1936, after which that type of changer was renamed the "World Champion." Very light and functional, it was operated with a lever located on the downtube of the frame, without the need of a backpedal. In its various versions, the Simplex—probably the first gear changer to handle a 5-cog freewheel—dominated the European market until the early 1950s, when Campagnolo abandoned its dual-rod gear changer to introduce the Gran Sport, a true Coper-

nican revolution in terms of the bicycle system. Today, the technical competition is between Campagnolo and Shimano, but in the years of Fausto Coppi the question was, Simplex or Campagnolo?

Campagnolo was always looking to the future, designing the evolution and improvement of his ideas, seeking materials that would make the difference when his products were compared to those of his competitors. A great deal of today's Campagnolo mythology came into being in part because of this constant desire to stand apart, this preference always given quality. Campagnolo operated for many years in the red because the metals he used and worked by hand were the most costly, but he looked on these losses as an investment in the future. So it was that in 1940—despite Italy entering the war and racing activity more or less coming to a standstill—Campagnolo thought it time to take on his first employee, hiring Enrico Piccolo, who had been the mechanic to Severino Duranti, a former racer, and who had the job of perfecting the ideas that Tullio sketched in his notebooks.

On May 4, 1940, Tullio Campagnolo patented his first

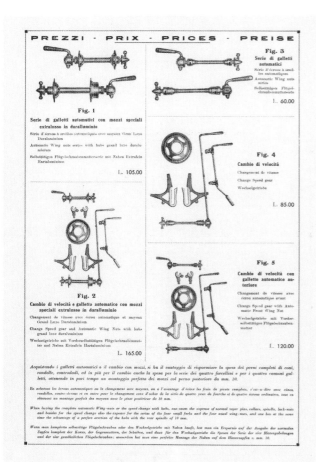

Four languages

A Campagnolo publicity flyer from the early postwar period (1946–50). Instructions and prices were given in four languages: Italian, French, English, and German.

version of the dual-rod gear changer, so-called because it used two rigid levers. One controlled the quick release of the rear wheel and the other operated the derailleur, moving the chain from side to side to the desired position on the sprockets. The secret of this device was the slotting of the rear dropouts, which permitted the wheel to remain constantly centered. Another great advantage, compared to those of the competitions—most of all the Vittoria Margherita and the Super Champion—was the elimination of the chain tensioner, which had been a great obstacle to the fluidity of pedaling.

Alfredo Martini, an old master of Italian cycling, professional from 1940 to 1957 and then victorious coach of Italy's national team for more than twenty years (1975–97, including six rainbow-striped jerseys with Moser, Saronni, Argentin, Fondriest, and twice with Bugno), recalled Campagnolo's invention: "Campagnolo's dual-rod shifter was the most ingenious of all; in terms of its engineering it was extraordinary. He had removed the teeth from the forks, so when you inserted the gear for the plain, the wheel moved back; when you put in the gear for the ascent, the wheel moved forward."

Even so, the operation of changing gears was still complicated and required talents not unlike those of a magician. In sequence, the movements to perform were these: operation of the longer lever to release the rear wheel; a backpedal and operation of the shorter level outward or inward to move the chain to the desired sprocket; repositioning of the longer lever and regulation of the tension in the chain; return to pedaling.

Often enough, the outcome of a race depended on a racer's ability to perfectly carry out all these maneuvers. A mistake meant losing time and getting left behind. "The Campagnolo gear changer rules out every possibility of breakdown and lost time," "Without friction and without chain tightener," "Without friction and without spring": so ran the newspaper advertisements. But many of the epic moments involving the great heroes of the golden age of cycling, from Coppi to Bartali, were often affected by one racer demonstrating less skill in operating a gear changer, or having less luck in doing so. "Coppi's on the attack . . . Bartali is losing ground." Yes, perhaps because the chain took its time finding the right sprocket!

The dual-rod gear changer

Quite clearly, having to get off a bicycle to change gears means a big loss of time. In 1946, a device made its appearance that spared the cyclist from having to put his feet on the ground. This was the Campagnolo Cambio Corsa, composed of two levers attached to the right-side seatstay that made it possible for the cyclist to change gears while remaining seated on his saddle. The first lever, located a little higher, operated the release of the rear hub; the second operated the chain-guide located above the chainstay.

Having released the rear wheel, it was necessary to pedal the crankarm backward to change gears. The tension of the chain was automatically controlled by the movement of the hub within the rear dropouts. These, designed by Campagnolo, were set an at angle in such a way that, when the chain became slack because it had moved to a smaller sprocket, the force of gravity made the hub move back to take up the slack. If instead the chain was moved to a larger sprocket, it was the chain itself that pulled the hub into the best position. Having changed gears, it was

necessary to operate the lever again to tighten the hub to the frame.

The later evolution of this system saw the two levers combined in a single lever. The rear wheel was released by the first 30 to 40 degrees of rotation of the lever, while further movement released the bayonet mechanism that operated the chain-guide. The operation was thus easier than with the dual-rod system, but there was still the need to backpedal to change gears. In a later version the chain-guide was moved below the rear fork, making it possible to change gears while still pedaling.

Variations

These images, from *Ciclismo Italiano* of January 1, 1950, present examples of different versions of the dual-rod gear changer. 1. The classic system using the backpedal. 2. Modified to make possible continuous pedaling (the chain-guide is positioned below the rear fork). 3. The changer with two rods and the "Ghisallo" application that made continuous pedaling possible also using this system. These various applications made it possible for the dual-rod changer to remain in use quite a long time and despite the appearance of more modern versions, although those also were heavier.

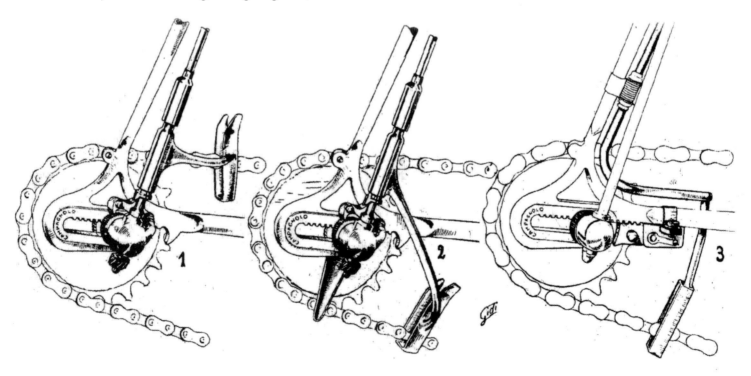

1946

Cap with regulation screws

The cap on the end of the axle opposite the quick-release lever is fitted with two screws that control the amount of pressure applied to hub on the basis of the width of the dropouts and the amount of pressure desired by the cyclist.

The tension spring helped the operation of the lever controlling the rear derailleur.

The chain-guide is the most important part of the system. This device moved the chain from side to side over the gears.

The closing mechanism is designed to permit the hub the movement necessary to keep the chain at the ideal tension.

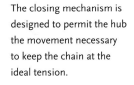

Quick-release rod

The quick release is directly operated by the lever attached to the right-side seatstay.

The name, the brand: communicating Campagnolo

Gianni Brera

The young Gianni Brera as a journalist following the Giro d'Italia in 1952.

A complex man, Tullio Campagnolo. He was humble, like many simple people, and preferred to speak in the Vicenza dialect. Even so, such was his determination and his stubbornness that in public he could seem authoritarian to the point of being despotic. For these reasons, he has been compared to the great car-maker Enzo Ferrari. Campagnolo had an enormous charge of human understanding and common sense. He was tenacious, far-sighted, and gifted with excellent intuition. His inborn peasant shrewdness was combined a lively mentality, making him a great communicator when promoting his products and his brand.

In 1948, when Vittorio De Sica was shooting his famous film *Bicycle Thieves*, Campagnolo managed to have racing bicycles equipped with his new Cambio Corsa appear in several scenes. And when, on June 6 of that same year, the Giro d'Italia included Vicenza in a stage—naturally in response to an invitation immediately accepted by the *Gazzetta dello Sport* organizers—Tullio received the crowd with people skills worthy of an expert public relations manager. This is indicated in a few lines from a sports newspaper of the time: "Tullio Campagnolo is a credit to his home town, welcoming officials and

journalists in his new plant, where he offered everyone a vermouth and a bag of exquisite regional specialties." All this was done to favorably dispose them toward the real reason for the invitation: "Campagnolo then displayed and illustrated the new derailleur speed changer with a single lever that makes it possible to change gears while pedaling forward and to move the chain from the smallest to the largest sprocket. It is a jewel of a mechanism that amazes those who are expert in the subject."

His seriousness and professionalism, his genuine, unselfish passion for cycling, earned him the respect and the friendship of the "men in suits" of cycling, the race directors of the Giro and the Tour, along with all the most popular journalists, those of *L'Équipe*, the *Gazzetta dello Sport*, *Lo Sport Illustrato*, and *Calcio e Ciclismo Illustrato*. At the races, he was always invited aboard the most important cars—that of Jacques Goddet, director of the Tour de France, or that of Giuseppe Ambrosini, director of the Giro d'Italia—and was treated with warm-hearted friendship. He became close friends with some of the great

Caricatures and jokes

Campagnolo became so popular during the early 1950s that the name and product became the subject of jokes, such as this one published in the *Guerin Sportivo* of 1953, during a period when Vicenza was part of a stage in the Giro d'Italia:

Vicenza, everyone knows, is very proud of its illustrious son Tullio Campagnolo. The following anecdote gives an idea of how true this is. It is said that after the Giro left Vicenza, a Spanish racer looking to change some money spotted a shop displaying the sign "cambio." He went in, showed his *pesetas* to an employee, and asked, *"Usted tiene el cambio espagnolo?"*

"No," responded the other. *"Aqui solo cambio Campagnolo."*

The caricature is by the journalist and designer Carlo Bergoglio, known to everyone by his signature, Carlin.

Bicycle Thieves

Visible in several scenes from the Vittoria De Sica movie, filmed in 1948, are bicycles equipped with the Campagnolo Cambio Corsa.

journalists of the period—from Guido Giardini to Emilio Colombo, from Emilio De Martino to Carlin Bergoglio and Indro Montanelli—thanks to reciprocal esteem as well as to shared passions and interests: hunting, for example, and fine wine. The leading Italian sports journalist, Gianni Brera, shared these passions with Tullio, and also shared his peasant roots. He became one of Tullio's closest and most steady friends. On the occasion of the sixtieth anniversary of the foundation of the company and the tenth anniversary of Tullio's death, Brera was asked to write a biography of his friend for a limited edition, not-for-sale, book. *The Giant and the File* became a cult favorite also because, through a trick of fate, it was among the last works of the writer-journalist, who died in a car accident in December 1992, before the publication of the book in 1993.

Campagnolo proved early on that he understood the world of communication, as when he painted the company name and address on the hardware store's cart. On January 12, 1946, he registered a logo to better identify his products: a winged wheel with the quick release depicted with the words "Cambio Campagnolo." He reworked the logo two years later and in 1953 launched the famous version with his signature reproduced over a world map with the words "Brevetti Internazionali." The logo was designed by the *cavalier* Pittarlin, a Veneto painter passionate about cycling as well as president of the Comitato Regionale Veneto of the cycling federation, which Campagnolo himself joined in 1952.

At the same time, Tullio undertook various initiatives

Catalog no. 13

From the 1950s to today, Campagnolo catalogs have regularly presented the new products being released.

Campagnolo's sign

When, early in the 1980s, the plant in Corso Padova proved too small for the company's expanding activity, Tullio Campagnolo made a strategic decision concerning the location for the new plant, choosing a stretch of Via della Chimica in an area highly visible from the autostrada. Anyone passing on the highly trafficked Milano–Venice motorway could not help but see the 40-meter-long sign reading "Campagnolo." Tullio himself was quite proud of it.

to increase his company's standing. He sponsored many local cycling shows and societies (in 1952 the Unione Ciclistica Vicenza-Campagnolo was created); he put ads in newspapers; and he carried out advertising himself, traveling from race to race to stay near the racers. Bartali, Coppi, and Magni, the leading champions in Italy during the postwar period, were the outstanding testimonials to his creativity. Five years after the end of the war, this enormous labor of self-promotion had given copious and extraordinary fruit—by then the Campagnolo company had 123 employees, which ten years later grew to 300. In 1953 Campagnolo published a 24-page catalog that illustrated, aside from the successes won by Bartali and Coppi, the Cambio Corsa, the Roubaix, the Sport and Gran Sport, each of which was guaranteed to "function perfectly" over a long life. The catalog also included the notice that, "On request, gear changers can be supplied with longer levers for use on touring bikes." Tullio was expanding his activity.

Of course, the reason for all this success was not advertising skills but sheer quality. Campagnolo aimed for perfection. Those who knew Tullio said he invented his products, built them, then broke them open to find their defects and improved them. If someone, astonished by

the quality of his components, asked him where he found his inspiration, his answer was likely to be, "All I do is make use of what the Eternal Father put in my head." His motto: "Meet deadlines. If you make a promise, keep it." He went out in person to see if new products worked the way they were supposed to, asking opinions and suggestions from mechanics and racers. If he learned that something about a Campagnolo product did not work perfectly, he immediately set off to check the problem in person, whether in France or Spain or anywhere else.

It has been written that Tullio Campagnolo was "more than anyone else, probably the one individual who had the greatest influence on the history of cycling." Aside from what it says about Tullio's accomplishment, this statement reveals something about the personal charisma he acquired. When in 1979 Julio Marquevich, president of Campagnolo USA, went to Italy for the first time to meet Campagnolo, who had recently been honored by the president of the republic with the title of *Cavaliere del Lavoro*, he said, "I felt like a gnat in the presence of an elephant." Only a few minutes later, however, Marquevich felt "relaxed and at ease," a fine indication of the kind of man Campagnolo was.

Campagnolo logos

The importance of the emblem

With his innate talent for communication, Tullio always gave great importance to the logos of his products. He turned to the painter Pittarlin for design of the Campagnolo logo featuring the unmistakable italic writing that still distinguishes the brand. Other recurrent motifs are the planisphere and the rainbow of the world championship, both of which emphasize the company's international stance.

Everyone for Tullio, Tullio for everyone

Tullio Campagnolo, former racer but most of all great athlete, had the all-important intuition to directly connect his business activity to the world of bicycle racing, and to do so from the very start. The successes of champions became the finest advertisements for the products bearing his name. And the racers themselves, from great champions to domestiques in the peloton, were the best sources for suggestions on how to improve Campagnolo's products; only an expert and demanding client who uses a product under the real conditions of races can provide the kind of information needed to adjust designs and mechanical solutions so that they will be perfect in every technical detail. Today, the Campagnolo company possesses the most advanced computer software and the most sophisticated devices for product evaluation—yet even so, direct and personal contact with the world of professional racing remains a fundamental part of the design and manufacture of every Campagnolo product.

Working for half a century in the field, Tullio Campagnolo earned the esteem and the respect of the leading champions of various eras. We have mentioned some of the first racers who, in the 1930s, joined themselves to the Campagnolo brand. Far-sighted businessman that he was, Tullio knew to be generous with those who were faithful to his products. There was, for example, Vito Ortelli, Italian champion of team pursuit races and highly regarded representative of the group. At the close of the 1948 season, Tullio gave him 100 examples of his gear changer, which Ortelli immediately put on sale in his store in Faenza. "He gave them to me," he said, "to repay me for the faith in him I had always proven by using his changer even when it might have suited me to replace it. Many things might have gone differently had I used a Simplex . . . but Campagnolo always treated me well." Indeed, when Ortelli got married—three days after the Giro di Lombardia in 1948, capping a season in which he had been Italian road

With Cottur

The Triestine cyclist Giordano Cottur, shown here with Tullio Campagnolo, was one of the most influential racers among the group of professionals during the years around World War II.

The 1946 Giro: Gino triumphs

Milan's Arena, July 7, 1946: Gino Bartali borne by enthusiastic fans following his victory in the Giro d'Italia.

champion, had won the Giro di Romagna, come in fourth in the final results of the Giro, and done five stages wearing the pink jersey—Tullio gave him a car to take his Giuseppina on their honeymoon to Paris.

Between the 1940s and 1950s, Campagnolo joined his name to the successes of Olimpio Bizzi, Mario Ricci, Giordano Cottur, and Toni Bevilacqua (much adored because he came from the Veneto). He did the same with many of the foreigners who competed with Italians for success on the roads of the Giro, the Tour, and the great classics: the Swiss Hugo Koblet, winner of the Giro in 1950 and the Tour in 1951, and Carlo Clerici, surprise winner of the Giro in 1954; the Belgians Briek Schotte and Rik Van Steenbergen, who together wore the rainbow jersey five times between 1948 and 1957; the Spaniard Miguel Poblet; and the Luxemburger Charly Gaul, the German Rudy Altig, and Frenchman Jacques Anquetil.

Even so, the Campagnolo brand is most closely associated with the epic contest between Gino Bartali and Fausto Coppi, which thrilled and divided Italians for a period of fifteen years, 1950 to 1965. Bartali, five years older than Coppi, has explained that during that period cycling

was greatly affected by the presence of four "aces" who had a great deal of influence on everything that happened. These four were Aldo Zambrini, commercial director of Bianchi; Adriano Rodoni, president of the Unione Ciclistica Italiana; Nando Tagliabue, owner of the Ursus tire company; and Tullio Campagnolo.

After his debut in professional racing with the Frejus team, Bartali, in 1936, began racing for Legnano, which used the Vittoria Margherita gear changer on its bicycles. Bartali literally dominated the field, winning Giros, the Tour, and major classics until the appearance on the scene of the 21-year-old Coppi, also riding for Legnano but as a domestique. Then came his surprising victory in the 1940 Giro d'Italia. In 1949, after the interruption of World War II, Coppi became a rider for Bianchi, thus beginning the challenge between the two champions that was also a challenge between the two historical bicycle brands. Except for the difference in their ages, the two carried on their competition with equal weapons: like the Legnano of Bartali, the Bianchi of Coppi had adopted Campagnolo.

Using Campagnolo's dual-rod gear changer, Bartali triumphed in the Tour of 1948, an encore to his success of ten years earlier. This was the same year in which Campagnolo opened a workshop at Cognin, in France, assembling and finishing bikes. Tullio had given Bartali the incentive of 1 million lire since his successes would help him establish his brand in France, meaning in the homeland of the Simplex. And Bartali had not disappointed. He had won seven stages and the final standing. The dual-rod changer was not simple to use, but Bartali proved himself an expert with it; no one changed gears like he did, or so it was said. He gave a convincing demonstration of this during the first stage of that victorious Tour, the Paris–Trouville, of 237 kilometers. The evening before, he and Alfredo Binda, technical commissioner of the Italian national team, had had a long discussion of how one might best carry out a sprint in the final meters. According to Binda, since the track of the Trouville velodrome was made of beaten earth, it was best to be the first one to enter it; but Bartali swore that he remembered instead that the track was cement and that he therefore wanted to have someone in front of him to open the way. But Binda refused to even consider this, so when at the end of the stage the compact group of racers began the decisive sprint, Bartali increased his rhythm to change position and put himself closer to the lead. When he entered the velodrome he realized, however, to his great irritation, that he had in fact been right, the track was made of cement. In that moment he did something extraordinary

that thrilled the more attentive of his fans: while moving ahead at full speed he changed gears, leaning down dangerously and operating the gear levers. "Fortunately I managed to change gears in time and without the famous Campagnolo lever playing on dirty tricks on me," he recalled years later. "And so I won in front of Briek Schotte."

This was the beginning of a long series of victories. Bartali ended the Tour in the yellow jersey and when he arrived in Paris Tullio Campagnolo was there to throw his arms around his neck. It was the final success, with the additional added note of that spectacular mechanical maneuver at Trouville, which stood as absolute proof of the quality and reliability of the gear changer. And did Simplex take note of what had happened! The next day a newspaper advertisement proudly proclaimed, "The stunning victory of Gino Bartali in the 1948 Tour de France is tied to the perfection of the gear changer without friction: Brevetti Internazionali Campagnolo."

That hug in Paris's Parc des Princes at the end of the Tour de France was destined to be the last between Campagnolo and Bartali. The great Gino, full of his success in the world's most important bicycle race, at the age of 34 and ten years after his preceding victory in France, decided in 1949 to form his own brand, to race with a bicycle different than the Legnano on which had pedaled for 13 years, and to train his own team. Thus was born the Bartali bicy-

The 1948 Tour: Gino again

Ten years after his first victory in the Tour de France, Gino Bartali, at 34, won it again, as celebrated in a Campagnolo advertisement.

Fiorenzo Magni: a lion as guinea pig

Among the first racers to put his faith in the early Campagnolo changer was Fiorenzo Magni, a great survivor of the golden age of world cycling. Competition with the two greats, Bartali and Coppi, deprived him of a sporting career more full of successes, but he came away with prestigious palmarès nonetheless, including three Giros d'Italia, three Italian championships, and most of all three consecutive wins in the Ronde van Vlaanderen (Tour des Flandres)—1949, 1950, and 1951—earning him the nickname "Lion of Flanders." Fiorenzo Magni, the great champion and brilliant businessman, today calmly pedals toward the age of 90. He is the president and also the soul of the Ghisallo Cycling Museum. As a racer, he was highly attentive to the evolution of cycling, sometimes taking on the role of promoter. In 1952, he convinced everyone in Europe that the time had come to introduce sponsors to cycling and became captain of the Nivea-Fuchs team, which for the first time wore a jersey that combined the name of the bicycle maker with that of a brand from outside the world of cycling: Nivea, a maker of cosmetics. This is what he has to say about his first Campagnolo changer:

"It was 1937, I was 17 and raced among the trainees. Aldo Bini, a famous Tuscan racer of the period, convinced me to put that novelty on my bike at a time when everyone was using the Vittoria changer. I was without doubt the first Italian trainee to use that device. Bini was a close friend of Campagnolo, as well as one of his great admirers. In effect, Campagnolo was an extraordinary figure and I had the honor of having him as a friend even after the conclusion of my career. We had a lot of respect for each other. He was brilliant, as proven by the heights to which he brought his company name; you don't reach levels like that if you're not outstanding, most of all if you take into consideration the fierce competition he had to face from other brands, most of all the French Simplex, which was highly rated in the post-war period. Campagnolo left nothing to chance. He tested and tested his inventions for a long time and wouldn't put them on the market if he wasn't sure of their perfect functioning. His gear changer was revolutionary because it eliminated friction and made it easier to pedal."

With clenched teeth

Magni raced much of the 1956 Giro with a broken collarbone. Unable to pull on the handlebars, he tied an inner tube to the bars and gripped the end in his mouth.

47

cle, obviously painted yellow. It was built by the Santamaria brothers in Novi Ligure, former makers for the Fiorelli company. Because of a lack of money, however, the components of the bike were not of the highest rank. Since he could not afford to put Campagnolo on his bikes, Bartali chose the most recent version of the Vittoria Margherita, the cable-operated Cervino derailleur, which cost a great deal less. But it was a true pain, compared to the Campagnolo: it was necessary to release the chain tightener, change sprockets, and then return the chain to the correct tension by operating alternatively two levers located to the right side of the downtube. The malicious claimed that Bartali alone knew how to work it, but in fact the changer caused him quite a few problems as well. In his memoirs, he recalls that he could have won the Giro d'Italia in 1950 if it had not been for all the mechanical problems caused by that changer, as well as by the Santamaria brothers' lethargy in bringing him assistance. They were in charge of the team car, and the brother doing the driving was nervous during descents and drove poorly on twisting roads. There was in particular the stage in the Dolomites between Vicenza and Bolzano, at 271 km. Aside from dealing with his adversaries, most of all Hugo Koblet in the pink jersey, Bartali was driven to distraction by problems with the changer. Although he went on to win the stage, he was unable to shorten his interval of 3'42" in the overall standings.

Koblet won that Giro, the first non-Italian racer to win the Giro. He raced with the Guerra team and was equipped with Campagnolo. Two years later, in 1952, at the world championships in Luxembourg, Bartali once again found himself cursing the mechanics of his changer. On the last lap of the circuit, the racers favored to win were all there: Bobet and Ockers, Van Steenbergen and Magni, Petrucci and Bevilacqua. In the ascent to the finish line, which was clearly in view, Bartali tried to surprise them with a sudden burst ahead, but while trying to change gears the chain came loose. The winner was the unknown German Heinz Müller, much to the surprise of the champions, all of them crowded together and keeping a sharp eye on each other.

Even so, without doubt the greatest ambassador of Campagnolo in Europe was Fausto Coppi. The Champion of Champions, as he was known, first encountered a Campagnolo changer in 1946, when he began competing on Bianchi bikes. He had immediate confidence in the Campagnolo device, which was being used by the team because of the close relationship between Aldo Zambrini, Bianchi's commercial director, and Tullio Campagnolo. It is said that the men had gotten along well from their first meeting. Tullio had grabbed hold of Zambrini's hand and said, in his Vicenza dialect, "Mi sò Campagnolo" ("I'm Campagnolo"). To which Zambrini responded, with good-natured irony, "So I see, so I see."

During the first years of the postwar period, Coppi, racing for Bianchi and using Campagnolo, won just about everything there was to be won: the Giro d'Italia, Milan–San Remo, Giro di Lombardia, Grand Prix des Nations, national road championships, and pursuit races on tracks. But at the beginning of the 1949 season, by which time Bianchi had already arranged for the team's bikes to use the Campagnolo Corsa changer, Coppi, in a truly dramatic turnabout, had chosen instead to use the Simplex. Coppi had been convinced to make the change by Lucien Juy, commercial director of the French company, along with Aliprandi, the Italian representative, and most of all by the offer of an enormous amount of money.

Andrea Carrera, a Piedmontese from Gavi, spent most of his career riding alongside Coppi, from 1949 to 1958, along with another faithful domestique, Ettore Milano, from Novara. Here is how Carrera remembered that

Tullio and Fausto, great friends

Over the years a special friendship grew between Campagnolo and Coppi, as indicated by this photograph.

period: "Even when I was an amateur, I always preferred Campagnolo; it was perfect, did not cause friction, and most of all never broke. My friend Ettore Milano used the Vittoria Margherita. When I went professional in 1949, with the Bianchi of Coppi, I found myself having to pedal with the Simplex. That was because of a personal agreement made between the French and Fausto. But I didn't like it and didn't like using it. I still remember the Cosenza–Salerno stage of that Giro: Coppi won it with a sprint. I was in the front pack, but in changing gears the whole thing came off, and I arrived with an interval of more than a minute since I'd had to get the chain back in position. In that moment I said to myself, enough with the Simplex.

Fortunately, Coppi himself was of the same idea, even though in the end he won that Giro thanks to his solo breakaway in the Cuneo–Pinerolo. It seems to me that already in the course of that same season, already at the Tour, which Fausto won, scoring an extraordinary double, something never done before then—that was when we went back to using Campagnolo.

"I had the great honor of meeting the *commendator* Tullio personally. He was an extraordinary man, and great worker, a genius, but most of all a friend to us racers. If you needed something, he gave it to you without asking for anything in return, he was sensible and generous. One of the best memories I have of him is the Stelvio stage of the Giro in

Carrera and Coppi

Andrea Carrera, nicknamed "Sandrino," was among the most faithful of Fausto Coppi's domestiques. Here they race side by side in a stage of the 1952 Tour.

1953. It seemed that Koblet was going to win that Giro and that Coppi had given up. But that night *commendator* Zambrini and all of us in the team asked Fausto to try to win all the same; all things considered, the interval in the standings between him and the Swiss was only two minutes. I still remember the scene as he began the ascent of Stelvio: Coppi did not decide to attack, perhaps he had promised Koblet, but he gave free rein to his teammates. Defilippis shot off and I got behind him. And behind came our car, following us and urging us on. It was a convertible Aprilia, and waving us on and cheering us was the *commendator* Zambrini and right there with him was Tullio Campagnolo, waving away at us . . . Then Coppi took off, it was like he was flying . . . He won the stage and the Giro and I did all right too, coming in ninth at nine minutes together with Ockers."

In the middle of that season, Tullio convinced Coppi and Bianchi to go back to his changer, which had evolved into a single rod. In reality, Campagnolo drew up a personal contract with Fausto, at a stratospheric price even for those years: 23 million lira over three years, to test the innovations, suggest improvements, collect opinions from colleagues,

and report back. And naturally to win. Coppi was the first to use an example of the Cambio Corsa modified especially for the Paris–Roubaix and thus called the "Roubaix" after Coppi won that classic in 1950. That same year Fausto, who, with his charisma, had a great deal of influence on the peloton, convinced Learco Guerra, an ex-champion of the 1930s who had become a bicycle maker and was commercial director of the team that bore his name, to engage the Swiss Hugo Koblet and give him a bike fitted with a Campagnolo derailleur. The elegant Koblet won the Giro d'Italia. In 1952 Coppi won both the Giro and the Tour experimenting with the new Gran Sport Extra; the following year he triumphed in the world championships at Lugano using a revolutionary modification to the mechanism. In that world championship, Tullio Campagnolo enjoyed a special, highly personal triumph of his own: First and second among the amateurs with Filippo and Nencini, and first and second among the pros with Coppi and Derijcke.

Thus it was as a result of the prestigious testimonial from Coppi that Campagnolo definitively won out against the competition in Italy from the Vittoria and at the same

Opposite
**The champion
and his bike**

Fausto Coppi inspects his bike before departing on a stage of the 1951 Giro.

Coppi and Roubaix, with a dedication

Victory and baptism

In 1950, following their brief Simplex experiment, Coppi and Bianchi went back to using Campagnolo. That year Coppi won the legendary Paris–Roubaix using a type of derailleur especially made for that race, a variant of the Gran Sport that, following Coppi's sensational victory, came to be known as the Roubaix.

When the 1950 season began, Fausto Coppi was irritated with journalists for writing that he was unable to win the great international classics. In truth, although he had won everything in Italy, at that time he had had only two successes in the Grand Prix des Nations. Coppi accepted the challenge and decided to play things his way. The ultimate goal of his early season preparations was victory in Paris–Roubaix, the most prestigious of the northern classics. If nothing else, his own brother Serse had won the race the preceding year, although in an unusual way (three riders had arrived ahead of him at the finish line, but without following the official course). For Fausto to win the race would put an extraordinary family double in the history books of cycling.

Everyone at Bianchi did his best to prepare for the big race. A few days before the departure for France, a special strategy meeting was held involving the sports director Giovanni Tragella, the mechanic Pinella De Grandi, and Tullio Campagnolo, who brought along a special gear changer. This was an evolution of the Gran Sport made to meet the particular characteristics of the route. It was a dual-rod derailleur but with a single lever and five rear sprockets. Pinella had put together a special bicycle with a reinforced frame to handle the different pavement of northern Europe. With Coppi were the domestiques Conte, Pasquini, Crippa, Milano, Carrea, and Serse Coppi. In Paris, when Pierre Chany, leading writer for *L'Équipe*, went to the hotel Regina de Passy to interview Coppi, he found him seated on a masseur's cot lost in thought while fiddling with a sprocket. While they spoke, a mechanic rushed into the room, snatched away the sprocket, and rushed back out: no one was supposed the see it. Coppi then received a mysterious phone call that informed him that past Wattignies the best stretch of the road shoulder was on the left. Coppi asked Chany if this was indeed true. Clearly, even the smallest detail was not going to be neglected. Coppi then declared that he was hoping for a close race in order to be able to break loose on the Côte de Doullens, one of the key points of the course.

The day of the race brought rain and strong wind. Favored to win was the Belgian Briek Schotte. Coppi kept to the middle of the pack, shielded from the wind by Carrea, Conte, and Crippa, who several times pushed him along to make the going easier for him. When they reached the Côte de Doullens, Coppi was in the lead, followed by Magni and Mahè, and at that point the pack broke in two; a little behind the lead there was Oreste Conte with his bags full of rice tartines and honey sandwiches. At a signal from Zambrini in the following car (with Campagnolo among the passengers), Conte made the effort to reach Coppi and passed him the food bags. This was the signal that something was about to happen. Diot and Sciardis took the precaution of racing ahead a few hundred yards. But Coppi suddenly exploded along the left shoulder. He changed gears and exploded again, then again put his hand on the gears. Within a few meters he took the lead.

The first to follow him was Magni, followed by Coste, Van Steenbergen, and Bobet. The motorcycles flew ahead; all around was excited movement. In a few more kilometers, Coppi caught and passed the two fugitives. Sciardis gave up, while Diot kept up until instructed to slow down because his captain, Van Steenbergen, was coming along with Magni and Bobet on his wheel. So Coppi took cover, moving to the area of the shoulder where most of the spectators were

1002 - CAMBIO PARIS-ROUBAIX CON MOZZI CALIBRATI **CAMPAGNOLO**

FAUSTO COPPI durante la sua vittoriosa Paris-Roubaix con il cambio che ha preso il nome della grande prova e mozzi calibrati con bloccaggi originali **Campagnolo.**

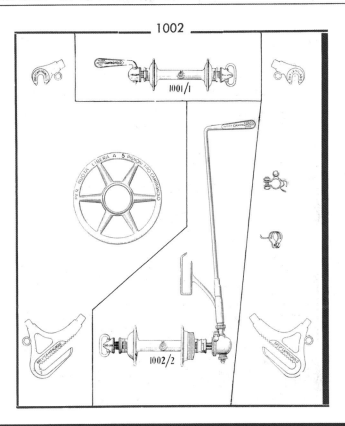

A RICHIESTA SI FORNISCONO I CAMBI CON LA MANIGLIA 42 PIÙ LUNGA PER CICLI DA TURISMO

NELLE ORDINAZIONI PRECISARE SE SI VUOLE IL DISCO PER RUOTA LIBERA a 4 o a 5 PIGNONI

crowded in, and then took off, leaving behind his companions in the sprint. Then he set off again. Three violent dashes supported by forceful changes of gear. He was all alone. Roubaix was 45 kilometers away, but his was an exultant ride.

At the finish line, the *Campionissimo* gave exultant embraces to Zambrini and then Tullio Campagnolo. Soon Maurice Diot arrived and began saying, "I'm the winner." To those who asked him if he'd taken leave of his senses, he replied, "I won because Coppi belongs to a different category!" To which the exultant Campagnolo declared, "And my derailleur belongs to a different category!" From then on, the derailleur was called the Roubaix. Any detractors who still doubted Coppi's power in the classics outside Italy were silenced a week later when Coppi won the Flèche Wallonne, earning more prestigious advertising for Campagnolo's Roubaix.

The Gran Sport derailleur

The Cambio Gran Sport, introduced in 1950, brought the bicycle gear changer to a level very similar to that of modern systems. The chain-guide was located below the rear triangle, and it was no longer necessary to backpedal to change gears. The tension of the chain was no longer controlled by movement of the rear hub, but was regulated instead by a cage enclosing two pulleys that guide the chain.

In the Cambio Gran Sport, the dual-cable system soon gave way to a 1951 system with a single cable and a counter spring. The spring was loaded when the cable was operated by the cyclist to move the chain toward the larger sprockets and was then released.

This system was destined to be part of the Campagnolo range for all of thirteen years, and with very few modifications. The early dual-cable version remained at the prototype stage and never appeared in the catalog. The control levers for the derailleurs, fixed to the right-side seatstay, were made with an aesthetic that was to remain practically unchanged for decades. Very few changes were made to these levers until 1985.

Campagnolo did not limit his efforts to the production of derailleurs. In 1956 the first seatstays, headsets, and pedals arrived. The introduction of the crankset in 1959 meant Campagnolo was making almost all of what is commonly referred to as a *gruppo*, meaning the collection of mechanical components that make up a bicycle's technical outfit. This was a new and very important concept. The idea of the groupset was to become of greater importance in later years, with the manufacture of components designed to interact perfectly with the other pieces in the same groupset.

The complete gruppo

The idea of the complete groupset was taking form, with every component perfectly integrated with the other pieces. During this period Campagnolo also produced rear forks and dropouts.

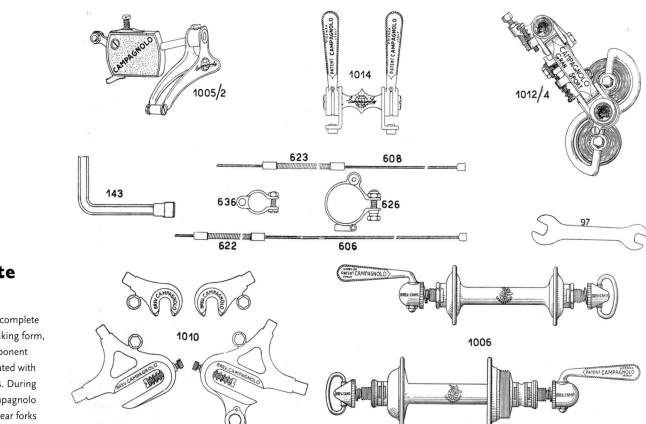

54

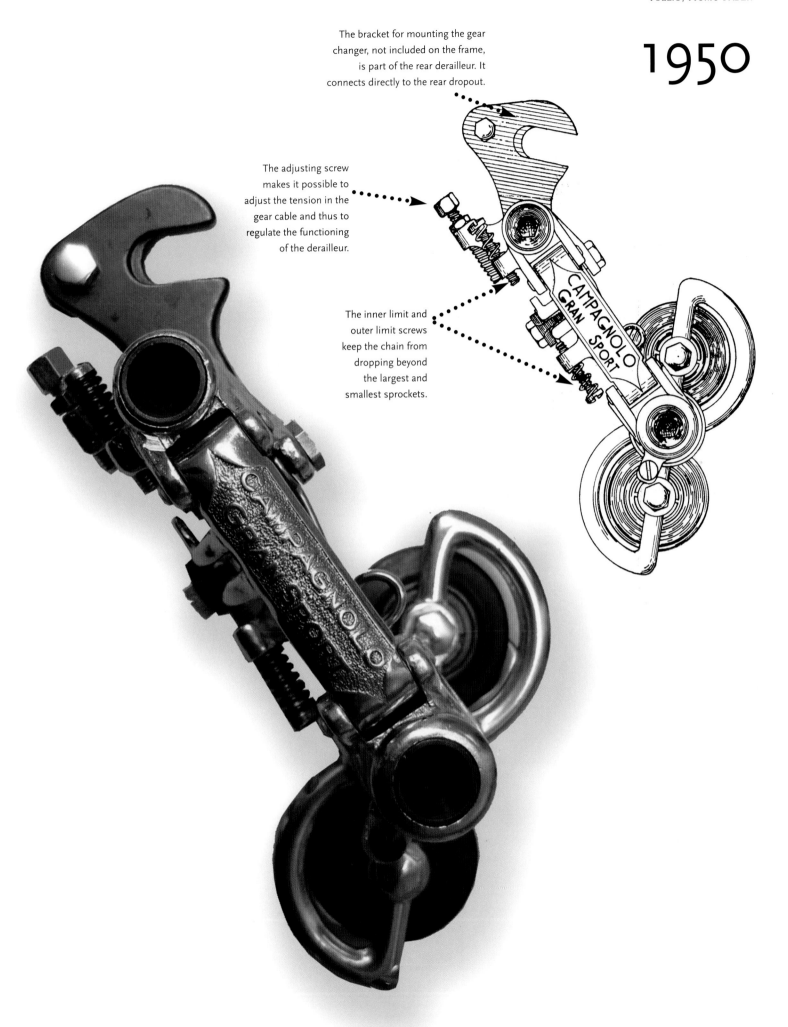

1950

The bracket for mounting the gear changer, not included on the frame, is part of the rear derailleur. It connects directly to the rear dropout.

The adjusting screw makes it possible to adjust the tension in the gear cable and thus to regulate the functioning of the derailleur.

The inner limit and outer limit screws keep the chain from dropping beyond the largest and smallest sprockets.

CAMPAGNOLO GRAN SPORT

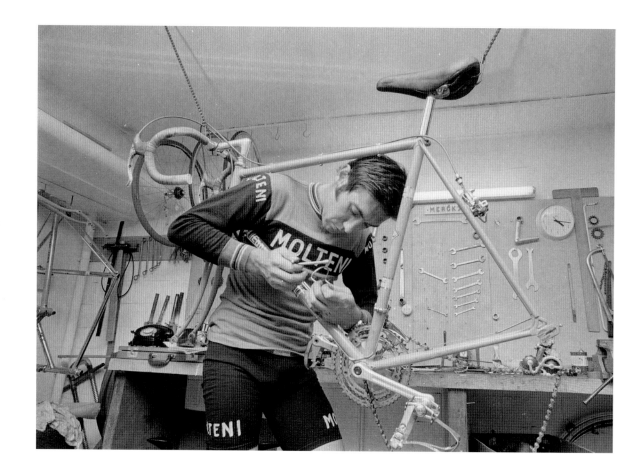

The Cannibal in the shop

Eddy Merckx in his garage workshop in 1973, busy mounting a bottle cage on his bicycle.

time affirmed its standing outside Italy, taking an important part of the market from such French brands as Simplex and Super Champion.

Even today cycling historians and fans argue on and on a question never resolved: who was greater, Fausto Coppi or Eddy Merckx? Impossible to say, probably, like all comparisons between men from different periods. One historical truth can be asserted: the victories of both men have in common their faith in the Campagnolo derailleur.

Merckx began his professional career in 1965 and from 1968 on raced with Italian teams (Faema, Molteni, Fiat). He rode many different brands of bicycle (Masi and Van der Est, Pella and Colnago, Kessels and De Rosa) but he always demanded they be equipped with Campagnolo components. It would be impossible and perhaps superfluous to list here all the successes of Eddy Merckx, known as "The Cannibal" for his insatiable hunger for victories. He had 466 successes in 13 years of professional activity, something like 1 victory every 2 weeks. In 1981, he went into the business of making bicycles. He remained faithful to the Campagnolo brand, and the bicycles that bear his name still use Campagnolo.

Hands on the changer

Merckx in a race in 1977, near the end of his career, when he raced for FIAT.

Victory at San Remo

March 1976: Tullio Campagnolo and Eddy Merckx celebrate the Belgian champion's victory in the Milan–San Remo spring classic. This was to be the seventh and last of The Cannibal's victories in this famous race.

On October 25, 1972, Merckx began his attempt on the hour record, then held by the Dane Ole Ritter, a great specialist in time trials. The attempt was made at high altitude, at the Augustin Melgar velodrome in Mexico City. It was a triumph for The Cannibal, who scored the new record of 49.432 km/h, almost 800 meters more than the preceding record; but it was also, and perhaps most of all, a triumph of "made in Italy" cycling mechanics. Merckx's bicycle had been assembled by Ernesto Colnago, at the time a mechanic with Molteni, and later a great builder of frames; the bike, which had required more than 200 work hours, weighed only 5 kilograms and 750 grams, but it was as strong as it was light thanks to the use in the frame of

special alloys then in the avant-garde: the steerer tube by Colnago, the saddle by Cinelli, the wheels and forks by Columbus, the chain by Regina Extra. And then there were all the components made by Campagnolo: gears of 51-52-53-54-55 teeth, sprockets of 13-14-15. "For the equipment," Ernesto Colnago recalls with a touch of admiration, "Campagnolo used the same special alloys used in some details of the OSO-6 satellite launched by NASA. I remember that Tullio made the hubs in beryllium, a precious metal that united light weight and rigidity and that he had procured in the Soviet Union. The same material was used for the pedals, which were stolen on one of the many occasions that the miraculous bike was exhibited to the public."

The sprint at Montjuïc

By half a wheel

Felice Gimondi beats Freddy Maertens in a sprint at the world championships at Barcelona in 1973.

asked. But perhaps too well. When the young Belgian turned to see where Merckx was—he thought he was right behind him—he was passed by Gimondi. The Cannibal, held back by the excessive use of energy, had not managed to follow in the route opened by Maertens and had been unable to deliver the decisive drive; he came in fourth, preceded even by Ocaña.

For more than thirty years, the two Belgian champions argued about it. Maertens accused Merckx of not having said anything about not having any more energy; had he known, he would have made a sprint of his own and probably would have won; the Cannibal accused his young companion of having set off at full speed to finish first, going against team orders. But there is another, more intriguing way of looking at this episode, one that was introduced by the French press and that Merckx has always denied, but one that continues to circulate. Racing to the finish line at Montjuïc were three racers equipped with Campagnolo derailleurs on their bikes and one equipped with Shimano: Freddy Maertens. That year, 1973, the Japanese brand had made its big debut in professional cycling, a reality that had to worry old Tullio, who for at least two decades had enjoyed something very much like a monopoly. When the moment came for that decisive sprint, Eddy Merckx, faithful to Tullio, did not tell Maertens that he had little hope for success in order to favor victory in the race going to a rider using the Campagnolo group, and in particular the friend of his friend, Gimondi. And thus Shimano's first great victory in the professional arena had been put off.

French commentators point to a certain exciting episode in Merckx's career that can be taken as an indication of the extraordinary faith the Belgian ace had in Campagnolo: the world championships of 1973, contested on the circuit at Montjuïc, Barcelona. All day long, Merckx had been doing his best to make the selection. By the last lap there were four: the Spaniard Luis Ocaña, the Italian Felice Gimondi, and two Belgians, Merckx and the young rising star Freddy Maertens. Merckx had asked Maertens to open up a sprint and Maertens had done as he was

"The world championship of seventy-three? It's only a fable, the notion that Merckx wanted to have a racer using Campagnolo components win," recalled the victor, Felice Gimondi. "He did not do any favors for anyone, didn't even let people beat him in laps. They say he wouldn't let his little son win when he playfully challenged him on a street back home. At Barcelona he was out of gas and without doubt was happy that his fellow countryman

Maertens didn't win, and not because he was riding Shimano, simply because Freddy was the young emerging star of Belgian cycling and his success in the world championship would have a little obscured the figure of Eddy. I won that world championship. I was using Campagnolo, yes, but I won because I was good and caught the right moment to make the necessary effort to win the sprint."

So says Felice Gimondi, another great of internation-

FELICE GIMONDI

G.S. **Bianchi** *Campagnolo*

biciclette · prodotti speciali

FELICE GIMONDI · VINCITORE DELLA SEI GIORNI DI MILANO 1977
IN COPPIA CON HENRI VAN LINDEN

On the track

Felice Gimondi in a six-day race at Milan in 1976 and, below, Francesco Moser, record holder in the hour on the track at Mexico City, January 23, 1984.

MEXICO CITY
23.1.1984
KM/H 51.151
RECORD DELL'ORA

51.151

CICLI **Francesco Moser**®

via Bolzano 43 tel 0461/992215 Gardolo – Trento

di Lombardia, Paris–Roubaix, Paris–Brussels. Like Magni dealing with Coppi and Bartali, he had the misfortune to find the Cannibal on his horizon. But Gimondi was faithful to Campagnolo: "I always raced only with Campagnolo, there was no alternative that stood comparison. Only once, when very young, I used a Vittoria changer, but because that day, I remember we were ascending Ghisallo, I had had to change bikes and ended up with the bike of the driver for my father's moving company who was following me in the race. Campagnolo was indispensable and those who didn't have it envied us. I remember the Olympics at Tokyo in 1964. After practice I leaned the bike against a wall and immediately a crowd of Japanese rushed up to take pictures of the derailleur, to look at it, study it, perhaps copy it. Tullio was a dragon, the company was his entire life. He thought things up, designed them, built them, gave us things to test. I still remember how he would listen so intently to our comments on the models he gave us to try out."

There's the saying about changing horses midstream. It happened, as we have seen, with Coppi and his brief "fling" with Simplex. And it happened years later to

al cycling between the 1960s and the 1970s: the world championship and Tour de France, two Giros d'Italia, and then the Vuelta a España, Milan–San Remo, Giro

Newspapers salute Tullio

Pages of leading Italian sports newspapers for February 2, 1983, announcing the death of Tullio Campagnolo.

Francesco Moser. After five years of being faithful to Campagnolo—in a nine-year career studded with successes: a world championship title, three consecutive Paris–Roubaix wins, a Giro di Lombardia—he "betrayed" Campagnolo for Shimano. "It's true," Moser recalls. "I had always used the Campagnolo groupset on my bicycles, in the years between 1976 and 1980, when I was at Sanson. In fact, in 1980 Campagnolo appeared on our Famcucine jerseys as the second sponsor. He was a great man, not only a genius at mechanics. You could talk to him about anything. Then in November 1981, when I changed teams, I was contacted by the Italian importer of Shimano who made me an offer. The Japanese derailleur was very good, it seemed to me to be even more sensitive than Campagnolo. I stayed with Shimano for a few seasons, but then I went back to the Italian gear changer in 1983 when I went to Gis, which was also sponsored by Campagnolo."

Moser continues: "It was important to Campagnolo to have world championships among his palmarès. And in 1977 he was with me at San Cristobal, in Venezuela, when I wore the rainbow jersey." *Commendator* Tullio was so convinced that Moser would win that despite his advanced age he took the long and difficult trip to be with him. "I won," says Moser, "and when we got back to Italy we all went to celebrate in the beautiful villa the *commendatore* had in the countryside of Vicenza."

In 1984, when Moser pulverized Merckx's hour record at Mexico City, he used Campagnolo components, but by then Tullio had been dead one year. Moser covered more than 51 km in an hour. He used a Moser bike, a brand he had begun making in 1979 that today still uses Campagnolo components. For the record, before Moser, beginning in 1958, all the record holders for the hour, from Roger Rivière to Ole Ritter to Ferdinand Bracke to Eddy Merckx, used the Campagnolo groupset.

A few years before Tullio Campagnolo's death, Enzo Biagi asked him what he hoped people would say about him after he died. "Let them say what they wish," Tullio answered. It was not overly important to him: he had lived his life with a passion, a passion for cycling and for bicycles. He had invented and created in order to spare racers the inhuman fatigue of the past and also to satisfy his creative fantasies. He had done something. And this was enough for him. He was at peace with himself. Let the others say whatever they wished.

In the closing pages of his biography of Tullio Campagnolo, Gianni Brera writes, "If the name is that of a cordial Veneto peasant, the imagination is that of a genius who may never have realized how great he was. He applied his pragmatic sensibilities during more than a half century of work, with no pauses except those dedicated to convivial pleasures, to friendship, to sport. For no less

Pag. 12 - «La Gazzetta dello Sport» - Mercoledì 2 febbraio 1983

UNA TRISTE NOTIZIA HA SCOSSO L'AMBIENTE DEL CICLISMO

Addio a Campagnolo il «re» del cambio

Si è spento ieri notte all'ospedale di Monselice, in provincia di Padova, all'età di ottantuno anni, l'industriale Tullio Campagnolo, il geniale inventore del cambio di velocità e degli accessori che hanno radicalmente migliorato la tecnica del ciclismo Ricostruiamo le tappe dell'evoluzione dei brevetti che in trent'anni hanno raggiunto le duecento unità e che hanno trovato applicazione in tutto il mondo e persino nel campo dell'aeronautica spaziale - L'ultimo saluto al compianto cavaliere del lavoro sarà dato domani mattina a Vicenza alle ore 10

Nell'immagine a sinistra presentiamo il particolare del cambio Campagnolo dotato di deragliatore. Con tre ingranaggi anteriori e sei corone della ruota libera il ciclista dispone di 18 rapporti. Nell'immagine a destra, l'industriale vicentino venne ritratto con una pedivella munita di due ingranaggi in materiale speciale che gli procurarono il superpremio dell'International Magnesium Association di Detroit. (Archivio «Gazzetta dello Sport»)

Una corsa perduta gli suggerì l'invenzione più geniale

Tullio Campagnolo fu appiedato da un incidente durante una gara per dilettanti nel 1925 - Avvilito cominciò a pensare a quello che sarebbe diventato il cambio più famoso - L'incredibile aneddoto dei 21 milioni spediti a Coppi

VICENZA — L'ottantunenne Tullio Campagnolo, il «re» del cambio, è morto nella notte tra lunedì e martedì, assistito dalla moglie Margherita Andreis e dal figlio Valentino, in una stanza del reparto di medicina dell'ospedale di Monselice, in provincia di Padova, dove da tempo era in cura da un amico, il primario professor Carlo Forattini. Era ricoverato da circa quattro mesi dall'inizio di novembre le sue condizioni erano gravissime per le conseguenze di un'embolia.

Tullio Campagnolo sognava di diventare macchinista e all'età di sedici anni aveva fatto la domanda per guidare i treni. Così giovane, si vedeva già la faccia annerita dal fumo del carbone e gli occhialoni a protezione degli occhi, a dominare le locomotive. Gli piacevano i treni più di ogni altra cosa. E all'unico suo figlio, Valentino, ne ha regalati molti, come molte erano le automobiline che popolavano la grande stanza dei giochi del futuro capitano d'industria. Tullio ha provato la gioia di guidare il treno, perché il capolavoro che gli avevano chiesto gli esperti delle ferrovie lo aveva fatto in modo perfetto, ma poi cambiò strada.

Diventò il Campagnolo-made in Italy in seguito ad un incidente che gli capitò in una corsa riservata ai dilettanti, che si svolse l'11 novembre 1925. Se non fosse stato appiedato mentre scendeva dalla Croce d'Aune, quasi sicuramente non sarebbe nata la Brevetti-Campagnolo. Da dilettante, Tullio Campagnolo aveva vinto mezza dozzina di gare di importanza regionale, ma quella alla quale teneva di più era la Astico-Brenta, competizione che patrocinò quando diventò industriale. Quel giorno, Campagnolo avrebbe probabilmente vinto ancora, se un incidente non lo avesse costretto a mettere il piede su di un manto di neve che aveva ricoperto la strada. Ava difatti staccato i favoriti Di Paco e Gay. Amava rievocare l'episodio sottolineando:

«Ero paralizzato dal freddo e le mani cominciarono a sanguinare, perché la ruota non si sbloccava. Quando tornai a casa, sconfitto ed avvilito, cominciai a pensare a quello che col trascorrere del tempo divenne il cambio, consentitemi di dirlo, più perfetto del mondo».

Depositò il primo dei suoi duecento brevetti (con trecento estensioni in tutti i principali Paesi del mondo) l'8 febbraio 1930. Il suo primo cambio lo presentò nel 1933: un cambio realizzato interamente nel retrobottega di ferramenta del padre Valentino. Soltanto tre anni più tardi, però, si parlò del cambio Campagnolo come del cambio che avrebbe rivoluzionato il ciclismo. Il primo dipendente lo assunse nel 1940. La produzione in serie fu in grado d'iniziarla nel 1947. Da Raffaele Di Paco a Fausto Coppi: potrebbe essere il titolo della storia che un giorno l'amico volle farci, per rievocare le tappe della sua geniale e fortunata carriera di costruttore.

All'inizio lavorò in perdita perché il materiale che usava era indiscutibilmente il più costoso. Poi, quando si affermò in campo mondiale, conquistò il mercato pur vendendo a prezzi altissimi. Ci fu chi disse, dopo che aveva collaborato con successo con i tecnici della Nasa per i voli spaziali, che il suo materiale avrebbe fatto bella figura anche nelle vetrine di Tiffany a New York.

Quando concluse un contratto triennale con Coppi, gli inviò un assegno di ventun milioni. Il campionissimo non notò che la busta veniva da Vicenza e la lasciò ammucchiata in mezzo a quelle dei suoi tifosi che gli chiedevano fotografie. Soltanto dopo tre mesi, quando Coppi trovò l'industriale gli chiese timidamente se fosse disposto a suggellare l'accordo con il versamento del-

la somma pattuita, Campagnolo scoppiò in una risata e disse: «Si vede proprio che lei non sa dove mettere i quattrini». Coppi ci rimase male perché, in effetti, trovò l'assegno con dentro l'assegno (che oggi sarebbe di poco inferiore al mezzo miliardo) in mezzo a quelle dei cacciatori di fotografie e di autografi.

Il giorno che l'invitammo a spiegare i segreti del suo successo, Campagnolo raccontò che a parlare con i meccanici ci andava lui e non il capo officina. E quando qualcosa non andava, interveniva di persona e immediatamente. Un anno giunse in aereo al Tour perché gli comunicarono che uno dei campioni che usano il suo materiale era rimasto appiedato a causa della rottura di una pedivella. Volle la pedivella, la fece esaminare e risultò che era stata limata per danneggiare l'atleta che era uno dei favoriti del Tour.

In occasione dei mondiali di due anni orsono a Praga, gli domandarono quale fosse, alla sua età, la gioia che voleva ricordare prima delle molte che aveva provato in mezzo secolo. Rispose: «Il sapere che mio figlio Valentino è in grado di continuare l'opera che io ho iniziato».

Rino Negri

Novembre 1925. Tullio Campagnolo solo al comando di una corsa riservata ai dilettanti sulla strada coperta di neve.

than half a century he influenced and directed European cycling, from Di Paco to Magni, from Bartali to Coppi, from Adorni to Gimondi to Eddy Merckx."

In Vicenza, February 2, 1983, at ten o'clock in the morning, all the world of sport was present for the funeral of Tullio Campagnolo. An immense crowd gathered, and everyone was keenly aware of the importance and the accomplishments of the man they had come to salute. It fell to Eddy Merckx—the greatest of them all, also the most faithful—to deliver the final eulogy. The text was in Italian, and the Belgian champion read the words with tears in his eyes: "Dear Commendator Campagnolo, on behalf of cyclists all over the world, those famous and those less known, from the courtyard of this church I send you my heartfelt goodbye. You deserve to remain in our memories forever because—a racer just like us—you

knew before us our fatigues and you helped us. With your generous intelligence, you made us a gift of something that was the fruit of your abilities as a man and as a businessman. You were the most valuable and the most steadfast of our assistants. You came in first seven times, with me, in the Milano–San Remo; you were with me, in the snow, the day I climbed to victory along the road of the Tre Cime of Lavaredo. Every one of my successes I shared with you. In saying goodbye to you in the name of all those present and those who are no longer among us, I want to repeat a statement of faith: You will be with us, the racers of all ages and all classes, as the dear and unforgettable companion of the road. A good friend. Perhaps I speak in poor Italian, but it is with an Italian heart because, thanks to you, there is a piece of Italy bearing your name on every bicycle in the world. We will always remember you."

Forging the Legend

Postwar Italy:
a miracle from
the ruins

The "Made in
Italy" clan

From roads to outer
space, from pedals
to satellites

The discovery of
America, the assault
from Japan

*During the postwar period, a
great company took form and
grew around the powerful figure of
Tullio Campagnolo. Starting as
an artisan workshop, it became a
major industrial undertaking. All
of Italy was flourishing during
that period, in particular the area
devoted to bicycle products, but
Campagnolo seemed to have one
more gear than everyone else . . .*

Postwar Italy:
a miracle from the ruins

Italy in the immediate postwar period was a heap of ruins, houses torn by bombs, streets leading nowhere. The destruction of Vicenza, the city of Campagnolo, had been total: in November 1944 and again in the spring of 1945, Allied bombardments had smashed the historic center, the 12th-century Torre Bissara, the Palladian basilica. People wandered through the ruins lost, gazing with curiosity or indifference on the American, British, and New Zealand soldiers who marched through, leaving behind chewing gum and chocolate bars. Italy was a country without running water. Nor was there any gas. And there was no transportation. Eighty percent of the roads were impassible, 8,000 bridges had been destroyed along with 25 kilometers of tunnels. Eighty percent of the electric lines were down, 60 percent of the locomotives and freight cars were unusable along with fully 90 percent of the passenger cars.

Food, still being rationed, was hard to come by. Those who had a bike went off in search of oil, flour, meat. The price of bread equaled a laborer's daily salary. The currency in use was Am-lire (Allied Military Currency), and only the UNRAA (United Nations Relief and Rehabilitation Administration) made it possible to carry on. Fascism was gone, the monarchy had given way to a republic, but the war and the partisan conflict attending it had dramatic after-effects. There were episodes of vendetta, the day of reckoning had come: those who had been involved in the regime, even if only marginally, had to be careful.

The return to normal life was difficult, but there was a degree of comfort, after twenty years of repression, in refound freedoms and the end of the nightmare of bombs and shooting. In the midst of this chaos Italy sought to get back in order. Amid so much sorrow, ordinary people found the will to rediscover life. Theaters reopened, the taste for jazz spread, people danced to the notes of the "Serenata a Vallechiara." The newspapers were no longer censored or limited, requiring only the authorization of the Allied Military Command (permission from the PWB, the Psychological Warfare Branch), and they printed stories that until then had only been suspected, such as the behind-the-scenes reality of the relationship between Mussolini and Clara Petacci, or episodes of crime news, completely censored by the Fascist regime and now recounted by journalists with the air of a serial novel. Pre-war sports publications returned to print, such as the *Gazzetta dello Sport* and the *Guerin Sportivo*, followed within a few months by new ones, such as *Stadio* and *Tuttosport*.

The first sport to come back to life was the most popular: cycling. The war in Europe had not been over even two months when, on July 8, 1945, in Milan, the Circuito degli Assi was run; some claimed that as many as 50,000 people lined the route. Enthusiasm may have somewhat exaggerated the number, but it gives an idea of the great excitement that accompanied the return of bicycle racing. Fausto Coppi flashed over the finish line moving at an average speed of 42.5 kph. Many fans had never forgotten him and had been eagerly awaiting his return. As a domestique of Bartali at Legnano, Coppi had taken a surprise win in the Giro in 1940 and then, in 1942, in the middle of the world war, had achieved a new record for the hour at the Vigorelli Velodrome in Milan. He had then gone off to war and been taken prisoner in Africa. There were those who gave him up for lost. But he had made it back, although with a touch of malaria. The eyes of all cycling fans sought the figure, always familiar, of the great Bartali, the old Gino. During the war he had helped Jews by carrying messages hidden in the tubes of his bicycle, several times running the risk of being stopped by the Fascists.

On page 62
Eddy Merckx

The Belgian champion was always faithful to the Campagnolo brand. As a bicycle maker, he continues to use Campagnolo on most of the bikes that bear his name.

Fausto Coppi

Coppi riding . . . a Lambretta

The Lambretta motor scooter was a symbol of Italy's postwar economic and industrial rebirth. Here Fausto Coppi paces behind one during practice on the track at the Vigorelli Velodrome in Milan in 1958.

When Coppi was hired by Bianchi, journalists flew into ecstasy. When Coppi at Bianchi challenged Bartali at Legnano, it was the child prodigy pitted against the champion, the one-time domestique against his former captain. The future of cycling was being served on a silver platter. At the end of the year, the Giro d'Italia for 1946—the Giro of the "rebirth"—was announced. "The majority of fans," wrote Emilio Colombo, director of the *Gazzetta dello Sport*, "can't wait for the thrill of a Bartali-Coppi duel."

Still torn by the war and getting by in a makeshift manner, Italy took heart and united as a nation around this single thin element of cohesion, this emotion that was so fervent in both the north and the south, this passion for cycling and its heroes. This kind of competition was exactly what cycling needed but even more was exactly what Italy needed. It was all there: the rivalry between champions meant greater enthusiasm among the

people, which meant increased sales of newspapers, greater numbers of races, more money in circulation for everyone. It meant more profit for the bicycle industry and also for the artisans related to that industry, the people producing frames and components for bicycles.

At the end of 1945, the Officine Piaggio released the prototype of the Vespa, designed by Corradino d'Ascanio, who was later also behind the first Italian helicopter. This new scooter was available in only a highly limited number of colors, but its mere presence buzzing along Italy's bombed-out streets was a sign of hope for a better future.

By early 1946, Italy saw the return to life in every sector of activity. The first Ferrari came out of a small plant in Maranello in the province of Modena. The emblem on its hood, a rampant horse, was related to the family of Francesco Baracca, a heroic flyer of World War I. Around the same time, the first Miss Italy beauty contest was

announced. As a distraction from endless daily problems, Italian housewives dove into the imaginary reality
of the illustrated novels presenting such heroines as Di-
ana Loris (Gina Lollobrigida) and Sofia Lazzaro, the
name chosen by the Neapolitan Sofia Scicolone, later
better known as Sofia Loren. The stage diva Wanda
Osiris was already called the *Wandissima*; such superla-
tives were everywhere, filling a great hunger for exagger-
ation. Sport, too, was in search of a *campionissimo*, a
"champion of champions," a hero able to thrill and mo-
bilize the masses. In movie theaters, audiences were seeing *Shoeshine* by De Sica, and *Open City* by Rossellini,
masterpieces of Italian neorealism. The new actresses
from America were Veronica Lake and Rita Hayworth. On
May 5, 1946, Italians were offered the chance to get rich
quick, following the release of the first Sisal soccer pool
gaming forms. Guessing the results of the champions
would win a lot of lire and solve a lot of problems.

A true sense of important change came in the first
days of June 1946, when Italy held free elections and its
citizens chose to turn Italy into a republic. The whole
country was on a new page, at a new beginning. Even
so, the return was to be slowed by the ferocious dispute
between two opposing political ideals, liberalism and
Marxism, each of which wanted to impose its recipe for
curing the most serious ills of the country, which was
still suffering the effects of the war, first of all inflation.
The drastic action of the finance minister Luigi Einaudi
and assistance from the European Recovery Program,
best known as the Marshall Plan, brought the entire
country back toward health. The famous American assistance program was launched in 1947 and ended in
1952. Italy was to receive $1,515 million. Industrial pro-
duction, which in 1947 had remained stalled at 70 percent of the prewar figure, rose to 89 percent by 1948,

104 percent by 1950, and 127 percent by 1951. Over the
period of just four years, exports tripled, productivity returned to the levels of 1938, and in many sectors the
goal was passed.

These were the bases for what came to be known as
Italy's economic miracle. Hydroelectric plants were built
along with dams, the railroads were rebuilt, washing
machines and refrigerators made their way into homes,
there were the first experiments in televised transmissions, and everything in the construction sector was
booming—houses were needed everywhere. There was
an authentic boom in other areas of production, too: energy, iron and steel, mechanics. Everywhere was the
same fever for initiatives and undertakings that in a few
years were to make Italy one of the world's leading industrial nations, resulting in unprecedented well being.

UN CAPOLAVORO D

ANNA MAGNANI IN
ROMA CITTÀ APERTA
DI **ROBERTO ROSSELLINI** CON **ALDO FABRIZI**
una pietra miliare del Cinema Italiano

Neorealist icon

Poster for Roberto Rossellini's
neorealist masterpiece *Open
City (Roma Città Aperta)*, with
Anna Magnani.

Opposite
**Beauty makes a
comeback: Miss Italia**

The Miss Italia beauty
pageant made its return on
September 1946, at Stresa.
Viewers plumped for Silvana
Pampanini (standing, far
right), but the official jury
went for the less provocative
Rossana Martini (seated,
foreground).

The "Made in Italy" clan

The Cinelli workshop

The Cinelli mechanical workshop opened in Milan in 1946. Thirty years later, the brand represented one of the most original and creative makers of bicycles.

Italians eager to work, those with dedication and creativity, found themselves on fertile ground in which to plant the seeds of their fortune. During the war and for a short period after, Campagnolo had been forced to repair bicycles for a living. But now, with the return to racing, he was able to use his genius and begin making preparations for the future. In Italy, the field of bicycle gear changers was still ruled by the Vittoria, while in France and elsewhere outside Italy Simplex and Huret had the lead, but it took only a few years for the genius from Vicenza to win back his position and defeat his competition. The fact that Campagnolo was thinking about and investing in the future is also indicated by that the fact that, in the middle of this great period of initiatives, he found the time and the means to get married. In 1949 he married Margherita Andreis, 22 years his junior, and on Christmas Day of that same year she gave birth to a son, named Valentino in memory of his grandfather.

Campagnolo was not alone. It was precisely during the first decade of the postwar period that the generation that created the "Made in Italy" bicycle was born, grew up, and prospered. In part for generational reasons, Campagnolo can be seen as something of a founder of that clan. Whereas the others were just beginning their

The hatter and the Montagnolo

For every invention and inventor, there is always another genius who claims to have had the idea first. The opposite number to Tullio Campagnolo was Giovanni Mari, from Casalbuttano near Cremona. A hatter by trade, he was also a talented mechanic. During the years after World War I, he invented a bicycle derailleur that he called the Transalpino to call attention to its potential: it made it easier to scale heights, perhaps even to cross the Alps. Its ads presented it as "unique and infallible," "exciting and marvelous," "a highly modern and durable super-shifter for bicycles." When the Campagnolo dual-rod gear changer began taking over the market, Giovanni Mari perfected his mechanism, which had a single lever compared to the two of the Campagnolo, and Mari called attention to his version by using a play of words, baptizing his "the Montagnolo." Mari was more than just a gifted eccentric, as indicated by the fact that he designed a touring airplane, the Breda 15, and invented an openable airplane roof that could be unhooked in case of damage to permit a bailout by the pilot. Unfortunately for him, Mari possessed neither the business acumen nor the creative genius of Campagnolo. Thus his Montagnolo remains nothing more than an eccentric curiosity of history.

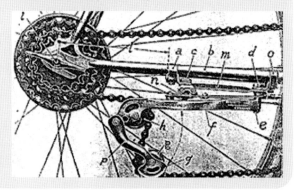

careers, for him it was a matter or relaunching the threads of an activity begun earlier.

Masi, Cinelli, Pinarello, De Rosa, Colnago. All were artisans who succeeded in transforming themselves into entrepreneurs. Their names are still legendary among bicycle fans throughout the world, and it is worthwhile to pause and examine them briefly since all of them came into close collaboration with Campagnolo. He was one of them, born poor, without much in the way of schooling, but full of creativity. Like him, they grew up with grease on their hands.

Cino Cinelli was another member of the "Made in Italy" clan. He was born in 1916 (and died in 2001) and was a high-level racer: he won several stages in the Giro d'Italia, the Giro di Lombardia in 1938, the Milan–San Remo in 1943. In 1946, he opened his own workshop. Like Cam-

pagnolo, he did not make frames but components and accessories. He made the first aluminum handlebars, the first saddle with a plastic body, the first toe-clip straps, the first clipless pedal. In 1978, he joined his name to the Columbus of Antonio Colombo, a company making tubes for frames since 1919, another piece of the history of Italian cycling, a supplier to such venerable bike makers as Bianchi, Dei, Atala, Maino, but also in the field of motorized vehicles (Moto Guzzi, Ferrari, Maserati, Lancia) and aviation (Caproni). During the 1970s, Cinelli was a major experimenter in aerodynamic shapes and new materials. In the middle of the 1980s the Cinelli brand introduced the mountain bike in Italy, under the name Rampichino. The collaboration between Cinelli and Campagnolo has always been intense, so much so that even today many models of

Cino Cinelli and Coppi

Cino Cinelli was a good professional racer between 1937 and 1944, but he made a name for himself when that career ended and he became a maker of bicycle accessories and components.

The Tailor and the Volcano: Masi and Campagnolo

A lily on the frame

The trademark of Cicli Masi. Since 1952, the Masi workshop has been nestled under the curve of the Vigorelli Velodrome in Milan.

Faliero Masi was one of the "Made in Italy" generation. Born in Milan in 1908, he died in 2000. During the 1930s, he was a racer of modest caliber. When he stopped racing, he became a mechanic for Gloria, the venerable Milanese bicycle company, and in 1949 he opened his own shop, which in 1952 was located under the curve of the Vigorelli Velodrome. For years, he was the trusted mechanic to Antonio Maspes, one of the greatest track cyclists of all time. Masi made frames with such majesty that he was nicknamed "The Tailor," and in fact his products were worn by Coppi and Magni, Alfredo Martini and Louison Bobet. Jacques Anquetil won the hour record in 1959 using a Masi bicycle. Between 1969 and 1972 Merckx used his bicycles, as did Rik Van Looy, Gimondi, and Adorni. In 1972, Masi California came into being in the United States, entrusted to Mario Confente. One of the leading models was the Masi Gran Criterium, which gained even greater fame when it was used by the actor Dennis Christopher in the 1979 film *Breaking Away*.

Today Alberto Masi carries on his father's great tradition of quality. He provided a portrait of Tullio Campagnolo.

"They were close friends, my father and Tullio, from back when almost no one wanted the dual-rod shifter because the Simplex was easier. My dad supported it, gave him publicity, and always stayed faithful to him," Alberto recalled. "Then later, Tullio was good to me.

"I remember him as a volcano. He sketched his ideas on a piece of paper then phoned them in to his engineers in Vicenza, saying, do this, do that. I saw how he did it with my own eyes. . . . Nearly every week he came to Milan; over at the Palace he had a room reserved all year. He arrived in the Mercedes with the driver. He never wanted to eat alone, so he'd call us over to keep him company. Then talking with my father, he'd take out a piece of paper and a pen and start drawing. . . . He had an idea every minute and when he thought it was something important he'd do whatever it took. In the world championships of 1968, at Imola, for example, Eddy Merckx had a Masi and was using Universal brakes. Two days before the race, Campagnolo went to my father and said, 'I made two new brakes, you've got to put them on Merckx!'

"'How can I do that?' my father started to answer.

"'Put them on him, they are without name . . .'

"So I asked Eddy if he wanted to try them. 'Fine,'

he said. He tried them and was enthusiastic about them, but they were still rough, without rubber hoods on the levers, and using them cut his hands. So on the day before the race I covered them in cork. And Merckx raced the world championship at Imola with those new Campagnolo brakes and everyone thought they were Universal! But you know how racers are, jealous of each other. So Adorni, who was with Molteni like Eddy, found out and wanted to use them . . . He put them on . . . and won the world championships.

"An example of his genius," continued Alberto Masi, "is that he made inventions outside the realm of cycling. The corkscrews, for example. One day my father and other friends went to the Campagnolo villa after going out hunting. Tullio tried to pull the cork from a bottle, but the neck of the bottle broke, cutting his hand; angry he immediately called the engineer and told him to design a corkscrew like this and like that. A week later the corkscrew was ready. It was my father who told Campagnolo where to sell it, in Milan, in a place that still today has the exclusive rights. I have ten of them at home! And then the nut-opener— not a nut-cracker, a 'nut-opener.' Campagnolo was

fond of dried fruit, walnuts, peanuts, almonds . . . and one day eating nuts and drinking Champagne he got the idea of opening a nut without breaking it. And then he invented the "Campastira," a device to keep a crease in pants, something highly useful to someone like him who was always traveling.

"Tullio was someone who never wasted time and had a very quick mind. There was the time Coppi brought some new crankarms from France, but they slowed down and he wanted to hear what we thought. We spoke to Campagnolo about them and one week later Tullio showed up with a pair of crankarms that did not slow down. Even the Masi Volumetrica 3V is an idea of Campagnolo's. In 1982 my father and Tullio were at the Milan trade fair and while they were eating their *cassoeula* they starting talking about the ovoid tubes then so much in vogue. Campagnolo said, 'But why not make bigger tubes?' And thus was born the Volumetrica, a true revolution in frames because for the first time oversize tubes were used. He was generous—even gave away ideas. When he made car wheels, I remember he gave me four for my Fulvia Coupé."

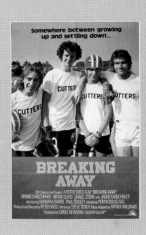

Breaking Away

Breaking Away is the story of Dave, a 19-year-old living in Bloomington, Indiana, head over heels in love with bicycles and with everything Italian. He loves Felice Gimondi, has named his cat Fellini, eats spaghetti, and listens to Rossini and Donizetti. Together with three friends, he takes part in team road races, but an Italian quartet knocks him out of the race by sticking a pump in the spokes of his Masi. This brings an end to Dave's myth of Italy, although he finds a way to get even. The film won Academy Awards and spawned a television miniseries.

The Record derailleur

In 1962 the Cambio Record appeared. The new model looked very similar to the Gran Sport, which it was replacing, but had an important innovation in the geometry of the cage. The new arrangement allowed for more precise functioning since the cage was more advanced and the chain had a better hold on the sprockets, thus avoiding dangerous jumps between gears. The work on gears also saw an important modification: the bolt circle diameter of the crankset was reduced, making it possible to reduce the minimum size of the smallest ring, which until then had been fixed at 47 teeth . . . From then on, the difference between the two front chainwheels was to constantly increase.

The market saw the introduction of a triple chainwheel, a development that in some ways anticipated by several decades arrangements in common use today. The cyclist was given even more choices for finding the right gearing for climbing a hill. The application of the triple chainwheel, which required a derailleur able to support the necessary increase in the chain's movement, was made possible thanks to the introduction of the parallelogram derailleur following mechanics still in use today that are decidedly superior because of the speed and efficiency of their functioning.

During the 1960s, Campagnolo components also came to be differentiated on the basis of production levels. In 1964 the Valentino gear shifter was launched, and during that same decade Campagnolo introduced a chainwheel made for cyclocross bikes and special components for track races that, in some cases, were also used in road races because of their lighter weight and the increased rigidity they can give bicycles.

Triple chainwheel

The triple chainwheel heightened the concept of bicycle gear changing and made it seem that there were no hills too steep for a bicycle. The range of gears increased, and the shorter metric extension made it possible to take on hills otherwise reserved for professional athletes. The image below shows a crankarm with a triple chainwheel for a road bicycle; to the left is a crankset for cyclocross with guards to keep the chain from falling.

1962

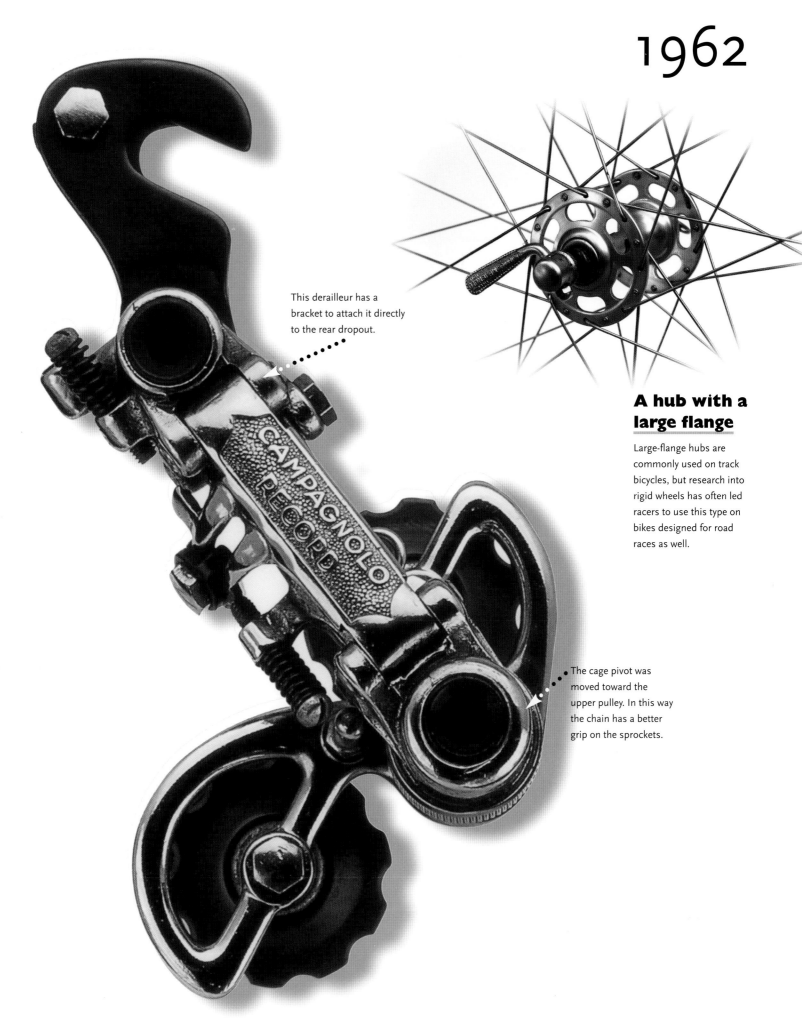

This derailleur has a bracket to attach it directly to the rear dropout.

A hub with a large flange

Large-flange hubs are commonly used on track bicycles, but research into rigid wheels has often led racers to use this type on bikes designed for road races as well.

The cage pivot was moved toward the upper pulley. In this way the chain has a better grip on the sprockets.

Pinarello: "We won it all with Campagnolo"

Giovanni Pinarello is from the Veneto, like Campagnolo, but belongs to a later generation. He was born in Treviso in 1922, the eighth of 12 children, and lived in poverty as a child. He was drawn to cycling from an early age, leading him at 15 to learn the craft of mechanic in a cousin's small workshop. He was also a good racer, with seventy-odd successes as an amateur and five as a professional in the period 1947–53. By the time he quit, he had already had his own artisan workshop for several years, thanks to 100,000 lire that Bottecchia had given him in exchange for not racing in the Giro d'Italia in favor of an emerging talent, Pasqualino Fornara.

Pinarello initially made touring bikes for men and women, and then dedicated himself to racing bikes. He soon made a name for his brand, thanks also to his close collaboration with Campagnolo. His first success was that of Guido De Rossi in the Tour de l'Avenir in 1966. That was followed by a long series of prestigious affirmations of his bicycles, including the victory of Fausto Bertoglio in the Giro of 1975, that of the American Alexi Grewal in the 1984 Los Angeles Olympics, the repeated triumphs in the Tour de France of the Spaniard Miguel Indurain in the 1990s, and more recently those of the sprinter Alessandro Petacchi.

Giovanni's son Fausto Pinarello says, "We're the ones who've won the most with Campagnolo: 8 Tours, 5 Giros, 5 Vueltas. And with Campagnolo we have had the greatest champions: Indurain, Cipollini and Petacchi, Marino Basso and Ivan Basso, Zabel and Ullrich, Vinokourov, Bertoglio, and Chiocciolo. Among the women, Pucinskaite and Bastianelli."

Pinarello is another fervent supporter of "Made in Italy," so much that he has an exclusive contract with Campagnolo. "Campagnolo is the best-selling groupset. Having an Italian groupset helps us sell overseas. We're Italians and we should support one another. The Record is the best. Shimano also makes a fine product, it's true, but we prefer to go with a brand from our home."

Miguel Indurain

Campagnolo advertisement from 1993 with Miguel Indurain in the yellow jersey. Thanks in part to his phenomenal time trial speed, Indurain won five consecutive Tours de France between 1991 and 1995, using Pinarello bikes and Campagnolo groupsets.

De Rosa uses Campagnolo

Bicycles made by De Rosa, one of the most highly esteemed Italian manufacturers, are equipped with Campagnolo components. This is a King 3 model with a monocoque frame in carbon.

Cinelli bikes are equipped with the Campagnolo groupset.

Ugo De Rosa, born in Milan in 1934, has an enormous passion for bicycles and began racing at a very young age. He became a skilled mechanic, and at age 18, in 1952, opened his own shop building frames. His name was made by Raphael Geminiani, a French champion of Italian origin, so enthusiastic about De Rosa's bicycles that he wanted Ugo to be his mechanic. That was the beginning of the unstoppable rise of one of the greatest creators of artisan bicycles.

De Rosa truly works with his heart, which not coincidentally happens to be the emblem of his bicycles. Eddy Merckx became one of his faithful admirers, drawn to his enormous care: for the 1975 Milan San Remo, De Rosa made five forks for Merckx's bike with different rakes, in order to have the one most suitable for taking on the descent of the Poggio. When Eddy Merckx became a bicycle maker in 1981, he had Ugo De Rosa spend time with him in person and help set up Merckx's new shop. During the

1980s, De Rosa went from being an artisan workshop to an industrial maker, with a new plant at Palazzolo Milanese, avant-garde machines, and excellent workmanship using new alloys.

De Rosa is another family company. The founder, Ugo. The wife, Mariuccia. And the three sons, Danilo, Doriano, and Cristiano. They are artisans, but few are equal to them in the working of titanium and, now, carbon. They have always concentrated on the quality of their product and have made a name for themselves in the world with their high-technology bicycles. They knew and worked with Tullio Campagnolo and are still tied to his brand.

Says Ugo, "Tullio never stopped! He became what he became because of his extraordinary passion for bicycles. I have always been loyal to Campagnolo, which was a decision of my own. If my colleagues had done the same, it would have been better for everyone. I'm in favor of Italian products, and Campagnolo was and is one of the best expressions of that."

Campagnolo and Colnago, the two knights

A helping hand

In the 1960s and 1970s, Ernesto Colnago was a highly sought mechanic always found in the retinue of great bicycle champions.

The "Made in Italy" clan of bicycle makers includes another member from Milan, Ernesto Colnago. Born in 1932 into a peasant family, at 12 he was an apprentice in a mechanic's workshop. Among the most highly esteemed bicycle mechanics—he was part of the Italian national cycling team—he opened his own shop in 1953 and began a career building frames. Soon enough, his emblem of an ace of clubs was appearing on the bicycles of grand champions: Fiorenzo Magni, Eddy Merckx, Giuseppe Saronni. Colnago made the bicycle with which Gastone Nencini won the Giro d'Italia in 1957, and those were Colnago bikes that the Italian team rode in the 1960 Olympic Games in Rome, winning the gold in pursuit. As the mechanic for Molteni in 1972, he built the special bicycle with which Eddy Merckx broke the record for the hour in Mexico City with 49.432 km.

Ernesto Colnago talks freely about his relationship with Tullio Campagnolo. "Tullio and I are the only two *Cavalierei del lavoro* of cycling: when his son Valentino sees me he always says that I remind him of his father. He was made a *cavaliere* by President Pertini, in 1979; with me it was President Napolitano in 2006. We were friends, based on mutual respect, even if I was thirty years younger than him. When he did something new, whether a derailleur, brakes, or handlebar stem, he always wanted to hear my opinion. I saw the vise he worked with and I understood his brilliance. Once— this was in 1966—he brought me a pair of new crankarms. I told him I didn't like them, because that was the kind of relationship we had, and he left them here. I still have them in a drawer."

The *cavaliere* Ernesto Colnago remembered the early difficulties of his career. "When I began work as a mechanic at Magni, I was 22; it was 1954. Those were not easy times, full of new things . . . It was a flight from misery, there were the first refrigerators, the television. I was as poor as a church mouse. At the Tour, they gave me 2,500 lire a day in living expenses. On the Giro, instead, I had to find my own hotel room and pay for my own food. So Bartali, Coppi, Magni had extra sandwiches made for themselves and gave them to me. To give an indication of the respect I had: when I was on the Tour de France, Zambrini, the commercial director of Bianchi, Tullio Campagnolo, and Locatelli, who was the representative of Campagnolo, always came to see me. They took me to their hotel, out to eat. They wanted to know what the racers were saying about the materials, the track. They respected me because in me they saw themselves when younger, the same passion, same enthusiasm.

"When I was at Molteni with Merckx, a Spanish groupset came out that was a copy of the Campagnolo, and they wanted me to mount it on Eddy's bicycles. I telephoned Campagnolo: he wasn't here, was out at the spa getting a mud treatment. I got in my Fiat 500 and went to him with the Spanish group. He examined it and got angry with the Spanish. And to thank me for telling him he decided to form the Molteni-Campagnolo team.

"There was a great spirit of collaboration between us, but sometimes it got transformed into a challenge. He had made a 42 interior and a 52 exterior chainring; I succeeded in making a 41 fit that same crankarm. Tullio heard about it and wanted to see it. He resented it a little: 'You could have told me!' But the two of us were allies when it came to dealing with foreign competition. Shimano, for example. I remember one time I was invited to a conference on production quality and quantity. There was a bunch of Japanese,

and I told them they were only good at copying. One of them answered, 'Yes, that is true, but we copy to make better.' He introduced himself and it was Shimano himself! He added, 'We'll show you what we're capable of doing.' I told Tullio about this threat, and he said, 'Don't be afraid, they're small.' But then the Japanese got big. Today I use Shimano and Campagnolo on my bikes, 50 percent, according to the suitability. The average bike I have made in Taiwan, but I have that written right on it, unlike a lot of others, and I use Shimano because it costs less."

Merckx's hour

On September 25, 1972, Eddy Merckx set a new record for the hour at Mexico City. He used a bicycle specially constructed for him by Colnago using a custom track frame and special components and accessories designed to provide the maximum in light weight: in fact, it weighed only 5.75 kilograms. As presented in drawings by Daniel Rebour, a great technical draftsman of bicycles, many of the elements, such as the handlebar, bottom bracket shell, and crankarms were milled to make them even lighter. The headset of that bicycle—the last with a traditional geometric shape to win an hour record—was made by Campagnolo with titanium caps and weighed only 122 grams, while the pedals and hubs were made of Soviet-sourced beryllium.

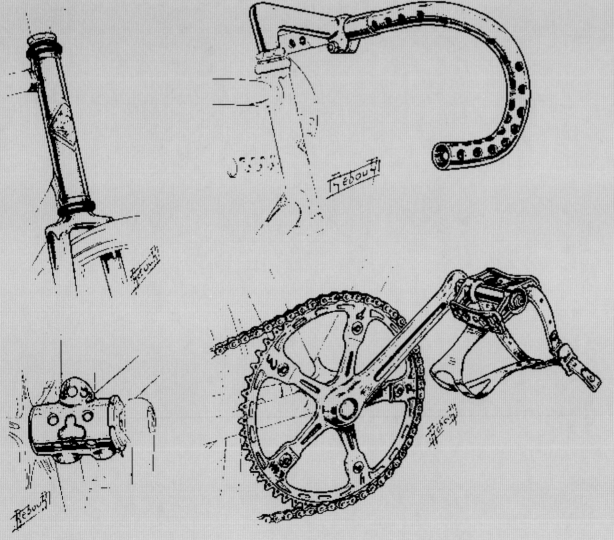

From roads to outer space, from pedals to satellites

In 1950, Campagnolo made its first parallelogram changer, the Gran Sport. It marked a big change, a new standard on which all other manufacturers had to base themselves. In the middle of that decade, Campagnolo introduced the *gruppo*, or groupset concept. The advent of the Record derailleur had been accompanied by a series of new components, such as the seat post, headset, pedals, crankset, brakes and handlebars, water-bottle cage, and pump holder. For the first time, instead of turning to external companies for all these parts, the same manufacturer made them itself with the advantage that they would better interact with one another.

Until the end of the 1950s, Campagnolo's commercial success had been reflected in an extraordinary flowering of champion racers with the consequent

kindling of a burning passion for racing among fans and the natural increase of interest among fans in racing bikes. The three superchampions of Italian racing were opposed by the two Swiss racers Kubler and Koblet, the French Robic and Bobet, and the Belgians Ockers and Impanis. In terms of uphill racing, there were the thrilling duels between the Spaniard Federico Martin Bahamontes, known as the "Eagle of Toledo," and the Luxemburger Charly Gaul, the "Angel of the Mountains." In sprints, there was the powerful Rik Van Steenbergen and fearless racers like Miguel Poblet.

Meanwhile, an event had occurred in 1951 that proved to have been of great importance, although at the time Campagnolo had not paid it much mind at all. To celebrate the new friendship between their two countries,

French friends

Part of Tullio Campagnolo's tradition was the maintenance of good relationships outside Italy. Here he is with Jacques Anquetil in the pink jersey at the 1964 Giro d'Italia wearing the team colors of St-Raphael-Gitane-Campagnolo. To the right is the German champion Rudi Altig.

Bobet at the Tour

Louison Bobet, on the ascent of the Col d'Aubisque, in the eleventh stage of the 1954 Tour de France. He is followed by Stan Ockers and Fritz Schaer.

Magnesium wheels

In 1964, Campagnolo opened a plant at San Lazzaro di Savena specialized in the production of superlight magnesium wheels for race cars.

Japanese and American cyclists had taken part in a series of races. In order to be competitive, the Japanese had imported French bikes equipped with Simplex derailleurs.

The Japanese have always displayed exceptional skill at making copies: they study the products of others, copy them, perfect them, and then develop their own ideas, often outdoing the original models. So it had been with wristwatches and motorcycles, television sets . . . and animated cartoons. So it was in the early 1950s also for bicycles, a sector that was experiencing an enormous boom in Japan. In 1945 there had been only 7 million bicycles in Japan; five years later the number had tripled. Various replicas of the Simplex marked the beginning of the Japanese industry in the technology of the bicycle derailleur: the factories dedicated to this specific product came to include Sanko, Cherubino, and Shimano. They were soon joined by the Maeda Iron Works Company, which had been making SunTour freewheels and hubs for bicycles along with agricultural machinery since 1912.

It was during the 1960s that Campagnolo the man began to fully experiment with his creativity and that the

company reached heights of popularity that would have been impossible to imagine until then. In 1962, exports to the United States began. In 1963—by way of using numbers to indicate the company's success—110 of the 130 riders entered in the Tour de France had Campagnolo

From two wheels to four

The Alfetta GT of Leo Pittoni at the opening of the Campagnolo Rally, an important test for the Trofeo Nazionale Rallies during the early 1970s. Behind the ceremonial starter Clay Regazzoni, a Formula One driver, one can make out the young Valentino Campagnolo.

With NASA

By the end of the 1960s, Campagnolo was so far ahead in the production technology of lightweight alloys that it became a supplier to NASA. Campagnolo made the body in Elektron alloy for the OSO-6 satellite, launched into space in 1969 by the American agency.

gears on their bicycle. The company was sailing from triumph to triumph. Its products were astonishing in terms of the perfection of their workmanship, the strength of the materials used . . . and for their decidedly high price. But the extra cost was worth it, most people said, because of that guarantee of reliability and efficiency.

In 1964, a second plant was opened at San Lazzaro di Savena on the southern outskirts of Bologna. The plant at San Lazzaro, with 184 workers, had a special function, having been equipped to smelt superlight alloys for the production of components of cars and motorcycles, principally the creation of magnesium wheels for cars. Campagnolo was the first company in the world to use low-pressure magnesium casting for auto parts, revolutionizing the use of that material. During the first years of the 1960s, magnesium was considered the metal of the

future, difficult to manipulate and for that reason not widespread. The Campagnolo plant worked out an exclusive technique for the fusion of magnesium that permitted the creation of perfect pieces.

Setting up all of this required a large capital investment and large sacrifices, but the results were thrilling. Making its appearance at the Turin Automobile Salon in 1966 was a Ferrari Spider with a Pininfarina body equipped with Campagnolo wheels in magnesium alloy; it awakened widespread admiration. Later, Alfa Romeo, Lancia, and Ferrari adopted Campagnolo wheels, which were mounted on the Ferrari of Niki Lauda that won the Formula One World Championship in 1975. The International Magnesium Association soon conferred upon Tullio Campagnolo its prestigious "Design and Application" award.

Campagnolo also associated his name with the

world of motorcycles. Early in the 1970s, the English motorcycle racer Phil Read was the first to use, on his MV Agusta, Campagnolo wheels. They were quickly adopted by other riders, along with various other components needed for the bikes. In 1975, for example, Walter Villa used Hydroconico brakes on his Harley-Davidson, winning the world championship in the 250 class; the power and progressive qualities of the braking enabled him to blaze ahead of his adversaries.

During these years, Tullio Campagnolo seemed to go through a kind of authentic creative furor. He produced rotors for helicopters, wheels for cars and motorcycles, and in 1969 made his entry into outer space: for NASA he built the aluminum and magnesium bearing structure for the geodetic satellite OSO-6, launched from Cape Kennedy to investigate X-rays coming from the sun and other celestial bodies.

After magnesium came titanium. Campagnolo was involved in the search for new alloys that would make his products more efficient and strong. The company was also highly involved in the conquest of the world of bicycle racing, which it most definitely did not ignore. By 1973, the number of employees at the Vicenza plant had more than doubled compared to ten years earlier, going from 300 to 681. By then there were also 225 at San Lazzaro di Savena. The earnings of 10 million lira in 1975 rose to 30 million by 1980, and out of 40 teams of professional cyclists, 38 were equipped with Campagnolo components.

A pilgrimage stop

A group of Vicenza bicycle tourists, on their way to the shrine of the Madonna del Ghisallo, the patron saint of cyclists, stops in front of the Campagnolo factory in Porta Padova. This was July 5, 1968, but even today many bicycle fans go out of their way to make a devotional pass of the Campagnolo plant on Via della Chimica.

Jerseys, champions, victories

HINAULT a choisi Campagnolo. Serait-ce par hasard?

Campagnolo support

Campagnolo was always on hand during the most important races. Here we see Tullio and a pair of mechanics in front of a technical support van during a stage in the 1960 Giro d'Italia.

Bernard Hinault

Bernard Hinault, a Breton from Yffiniac, dominated the international scene between the end of the 1970s and the middle of the 1980s. From 1975 to 1978, Campagnolo was the sponsor of the French Gitane team, and then of Gitane-Renault, of which Hinault was captain.

The 1970s and the early 1980s were years of widespread sponsorship and repeated victories: from 1973 to 1977, Campagnolo's name was on the jerseys of Bianchi; from 1973 to 1978 it was on those of Holdsworth in Great Britain; from 1973 to 1974 it was on the jerseys of Sammontana; from 1975 to 1978 the French Gitane; from 1976 to 1979 the Spanish Kas; in 1980 on the Italian-Spanish Zor Vereco Selle Italia, on the French Puch, and on the Italians Sanson and Sammontana; in 1981 Camagnolo was on the jerseys of the Italian Famucine team. And of course Merckx, Monserè, Gosta Petterson, Marino Basso, Ocana, Kuiper, Bertoglio, Maertens, Gimondi, Van Impe, Francesco Moser, Pollentier, Knetemann, De Muynck,

Hinault, Raas, Saronni, Zoetemelk, Maertens, and Battaglin won world championships, Giros, Tours, and great classics pedaling Campagnolo.

The successes and triumphs contributed to making Tullio Campagnolo the man of the moment, the emblem of "Made in Italy," earning him even greater fame. After the award from the International Magnesium Association, in 1978 it was the Stella d'Oro ("golden star") from the Italian National Olympic Committee, and in 1979 the *Croce di Cavaliere del Lavoro* conferred by Sandro Pertini, president of the Italian republic.

Atala *Campagnolo*

D.S. CRIBIORI FRANCO — PANIZZA WLADIMIRO — NORIS MARIO — DELLE CASE WALTER — BIDINOST MAURIZIO — FREULER URS — CASIRAGHI GIANCARLO — ANGELI PIERGIORGIO — ROSOLA PAOLO — RENOSTO GIOVANNI — GAVAZZI PIERINO

VITTORIO ADORNI
direttore sportivo
MARINO BASSO
campione del mondo 1972
FELICE GIMONDI
campione d'Italia 1972
MARTIN EMILIO RODRIGUEZ
"COCHISE"

G.S. **Bianchi** *Campagnolo*

biciclette — prodotti speciali

FABRIZIO VERZA — STEFANO GIULIANO — GIOVANNI MANTOVANI — PATRIZIO GAMBIRASIO — DANTE MORANDI — PIERO GHIBAUDO — FRANCESCO MOSER — PALMIRO MASCIARELLI — MASSIMO GHIROTTO — ENNIO AMADORI — MARINO SALVADOR — CZESLAW LANG — LEONARDO MAIZANTINI

GRUPPO SPORTIVO **GiS** GELATI *Campagnolo* TRENTINO vacanze FAMCUGINE

Teams and captains

Famous testimonials to Campagnolo. Bernard Hinault (opposite), appears in his French national champion's jersey. The Campagnolo name also appeared on the jerseys of the Bianchi team in Italy. This 1973 Bianchi-Campagnolo postcard presents the team's three captains, Marino Basso, world champion, the Spaniard "Cochis" Rodriguez, and Felice Gimondi, wearing the jersey of the Italian champion; with them is sporting director Vittorio Adorni. The 1983 Atala Campagnolo team included a world track champion, the Swiss Urs Freuler, and two Italian champions, Pierino Gavazzi (road) and Maurizio Bidinost (track pursuit). During that same year, Francesco Moser was the captain of the Gis Campagnolo team.

The discovery of America, the assault from Japan

In 1981, the company had to move to a larger plant, in the industrial zone of Via della Chimica with an investment of 10 billion lire. The new establishment was a jewel, equipped with the most sophisticated tools to design and build the most advanced products. "When technology becomes emotion" was the slogan that accompanied every novelty bearing the Campagnolo logo.

Meanwhile, something of great importance was going on in another part of the world. It would prove critical in the history of Campagnolo.

For a long while, Japan had been witnessing the progressive and steady growth of a company, Shimano, which year after year had been eliminating all of its domestic competitors: Maeda, Cherubino, Dynamic, Sanko, all brands that had satisfied the demand from a market in continuous and explosive growth. In 1921, Shozaburo Shimano had founded, near Osaka, the

Shimano Iron Works for the production of freewheels, and ten years later had begun to export them. In 1956, he had produced his first derailleur and in 1961 had arrived in America, attracting wonder at the International Toy and Cycle Show in New York. Four years later, Shimano appeared at the Bicycle Salon in Milan, studying Europe, studying Campagnolo. Tullio and Shozaburo met, shook, hands, and established a relationship of mutual respect that was destined to last the rest of their lifetimes.

In 1970, Shimano, already an unquestioned leader on the Japanese market, had diversified and enlarged its activity, extending its products to such sectors as fishing and golf. As for bicycles, it had begun setting its sights on the European market and in 1972 opened its first office in Düsseldorf, Germany. Most of all, however, Shimano intended to conquer the United States.

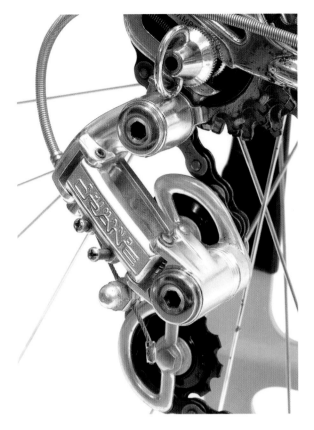

The so-called baby boom generation in the postwar United States presented a demographic blessed with well-being and drawn to the rapid acquisition of consumer goods, from cameras to radios to high-fidelity stereos. It was also a generation with a special interest in physical exercise, an interest masterfully supported by the shoe and clothing industry. This same interest led many consumers to buy a bicycle. In 1970, there were 7 million bicycles in the United States, of which 5 million were for children. There were only 200,000 lightweight racing bikes with derailleurs. In only two years, this modest number multiplied 40 times, rising to close to 8 million. In 1974, more bicycles were sold in the United States than automobiles, in part because of the oil crisis in 1973, a consequence of the ongoing Arab-Israeli conflict.

Campagnolo, Simplex, and Huret not had foreseen this boom in light bicycles in the United States and thus were unable to meet the demand. On the other hand, Shimano and Maeda had foreseen it all and were ready to successfully accommodate it. They provided products that were of good quality at a price far below that of their European competitors. Ahead of everyone else, the Japanese had also understood that they could save money by manufacturing the bicycles outside Japan. In 1973, Shimano had set itself up in Singapore and later built plants in China and Taiwan, as did Maeda.

For Huret and Simplex, the news was grim. The Japanese parts were equal in quality and lower in price. Campagnolo still seemed unbeatable for its light weight and the indestructibility of its components, but the high price of those parts often proved decisive at the moment of purchase. As a consequence, while in 1973 Shimano and Maeda held only 25 percent of the American market, by 1978 they dominated it with fully 90 percent. And the American press began to make comparisons, especially when the galloping inflation of 1976 doubled the prices of bikes: a SunTour Cyclone derailleur by Maeda cost $32, a Shimano Crane $40, while a Huret Jubilèe or a Campagnolo Nuovo Record cost $80.

That substantial difference in terms of the Italian brand was called "the Campagnolo tax," the "price of beauty." Many fans paid it happily, eager to have a superior product in terms of quality, but most buyers thought first of their pocketbook. Then, in 1983, the mountain-bike craze, which had begun in the 1970s, truly exploded in the United States. Once again Shimano took over the market. Having conquered America, and aware of its power, Shimano began its final assault on Europe, the land of Campagnolo. And in Vicenza, in that very same 1983, on February 1, Tullio died at the age of 82, after several months of illness. The family company passed into the hands of his son Valentino.

Shimano on the attack

Shimano's Dura-Ace groupset appeared on the bicycles of Flandria, the professional team of the Flandria bicycle company, in 1973. Among the racers on the Belgian team was the young and promising Freddy Maertens, who fiercely contested the world road championship in Barcelona that year with Felice Gimondi.

The Super Record derailleur

The year 1979 saw the Cambio Super Record in its most famous version. Indeed, the story of this groupset had begun several years earlier. The name *Record* first entered the Campagnolo catalog during the 1960s, so to distinguish the new model released in 1973 it was called the Super Record.

In its first version, this changer, derived from the old Nuovo Record and Record, was made with a single color available for the external derailleur arm, while the body was anodized black and made in Ergal, a superlight alloy.

In 1979 the Super Record arrived in two colors, with the writing no longer in relief. Because of its precision and good looks it proved a success. The details in titanium made it extremely light—it weighed less than 200 grams. The design was essential, its strength notable. It makes sense that this groupset, and most of all the derailleur, remained in production until 1987, by which time the futuristic C-Record had made its appearance. The last version of the Super Record groupset was distinguished by having crankarms without a central groove on the arm, but there was no change to the size.

The early 1980s also saw a first incursion into the world of off-road cycling. The phenomenon of the moment was called BMX, and Italian manufacturers saw it as a winning new trend from America. The market, however, did not respond with equal enthusiasm, and that area of the market quickly deflated. So it was that those manufacturers would be cautious in their first approach to the mountain-bike phenomenon. The prudence that resulted from their bad experience with BMX made them lose precious time in joining a new idea that, this time around, was destined for worldwide success.

Super Record, first version (1973)

The first version of the Super Record was very similar to the Nuovo Record. It is distinguished by the anodized body and has details in titanium to reduce weight.

Cage

The length of the Super Record cage makes possible a maximum capacity of 28 teeth. The Cambio Super Record was designed for six-speed systems, but there have been instances of its use with seven sprockets, an adaptation performed without too much difficulty.

1979

The new Super Record gear changer has an unmistakable look. The name Campagnolo is no longer in relief and stands out against its background.

The burnished finish is not merely an aesthetic touch, for it results from the use of a very light alloy.

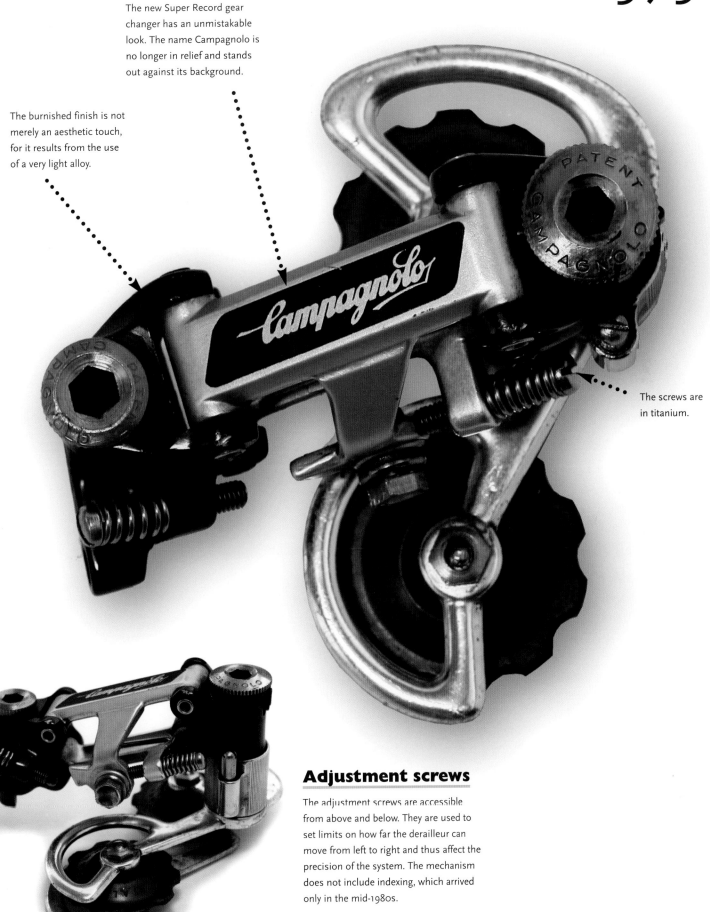

The screws are in titanium.

Adjustment screws

The adjustment screws are accessible from above and below. They are used to set limits on how far the derailleur can move from left to right and thus affect the precision of the system. The mechanism does not include indexing, which arrived only in the mid-1980s.

The Next Generation

The Valentino era . . . and Campagnolo moves ahead

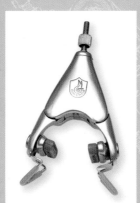

The wheels of fortune

Facing today's realities and tomorrow's challenges

Early 1980s: the turning point, as Tullio passed leadership to Valentino. These were years of powerful challenges and delicate changes within the company. But even in such hard times, the values that had been handed down—the humility and pride behind the name Campagnolo, the unshakeable faith in technological innovation—provided the roadmap and the stimulus for the relaunching of the company. The present and the future of Campagnolo share solid roots.

The Valentino era . . .
and Campagnolo moves ahead

**Record News
announces Chorus**

In the summer of 1987, Campagnolo U.S.A.'s newsletter announced release of the Chorus groupset.

On page 89
Ultra Torque

The Ultra Torque Record crank in carbon fiber.

To the truly faithful and most dedicated fans of the Campagnolo brand, it did not necessarily seem coincidental that Valentino Campagnolo—son of a father struck by a thunderbolt of inspiration while on the road at Croce d'Aune—was born on Christmas day. Dwelling on its possible significance may come close to blasphemy, but to certain fans it is only realistic, since the son has managed to carry on the miracle wrought by his father. Perhaps he has not done so with the creativity of a genius—that seems to have been the exclusive possession of old Tullio—but in its place he has made masterful use of the sagacity and skills of a true businessman. As Valentino himself says, "Like all the people of the Veneto, I'm a believer, I'm very religious, and I put my trust in the support of God for the continued success of my work."

Valentino Campagnolo has led the company since 1983 with the awareness of a manager directing a world-famous brand and with the wisdom and prudence of a peasant imprinted in his DNA. He says, "We Campagnolos came from a poor family. Life was hard. I remember that as a child I had one sweater that got tighter and tighter as I grew, so my mother, who could not afford to buy me another, lengthened it by knitting on to it, sometimes even using yarn of a different color."

Valentino Campagnolo has a wife, Sonia, and three children. He spends his days in the company head

What they say about Valentino

Magni: *"Valentino Campagnolo has carried on his father's work. He is very different from him. But he has directed and continues to direct the company in an exceptional way. You can see it in the results."*
Masi: *"We used to play with Valentino, when the Masis went to Vicenza to visit Tullio. He's smart too. All of a sudden he found himself having to bear the weight of an historic company. He had a few problems, but he has fully retaken any lost territory."*
De Rosa: *"Valentino found himself having to face the Japanese, he had his moment of difficulty, but then he took giant steps. And today the product is very good. The electronic changer is the most recent novelty. My sons have tried it. It's quick and will certainly meet with success."*
Colnago: *"We have a straightforward relationship with Valentino, he too is a great one. . . . Being the son of a father who is a myth is always difficult, and his strength is there in his way of doing things, being prudent and reserved. It's man-work-quality-family, and this does him honor."*

quarters on Via della Chimica when not attending meetings in every corner of the globe. He does not have time for hobbies. When someone asks him if he has the time go for a bike ride he smiles and responds, "Every day, from morning to night, and six days a week." Obviously inside the company.

In 1967, to celebrate Valentino's eighteenth birthday, Tullio launched the Valentino gear shifter. In 1995, to honor his father, Valentino assisted the Pedale Feltrino cycling club in the creation of the monument on Croce d'Aune as well as in the formation of the Gran Fondo Campagnolo, which today is an important annual event for cycling tourists from throughout the world. Dynamic and communicative, instinctively far ahead of his

time, Tullio had understood the value of communication; reserved, and a man of few words, Valentino follows in his father's footsteps and does so while meeting the needs of marketing.

Valentino Campagnolo is a balanced man, reflective and prudent. Also determined and tenacious. This is a result of his difficult beginnings. He speaks in a low voice, every word weighed and considered. "My father was a great man, but also a centralizer, not at all inclined

to delegate things. His life was the company, he did everything himself: planned, designed, kept in touch with racers, journalists. He was the company's director and manager. He looked after everything himself. He said: get beside me and learn . . . so I watched him work."

Valentino joined the company early in the 1970s, after a year of apprenticeship abroad with T.I. Raleigh in Nottingham. When Tullio died, in 1983, Valentino suddenly found himself, at 33, faced with the reality of

The plant on Via della Chimica

In November 1981, the new Campagnolo plant was inaugurated; the company left its old factory in Porta Padova to move into the industrial zone on the western side of Vicenza.

The Super Record 50 and the Corsa

In 1983 a gear changer based on the Super Record was produced to celebrate the fiftieth anniversary of the founding of Campagnolo: it included Tullio's engraved signature and the logo in gold. A few years later aerodynamics became popular—this was during the period of Moser's track record—leading to the Corsa model, with its clearly aerodynamic lines and modeling.

directing a large company. Suddenly leaping from theory to practice is no easy thing. Nor is it easy to step in for a myth. Furthermore, Valentino took over Campagnolo during years that were critical to the bicycle industry.

"During the middle of the eighties," he says, "the market for racing bikes had dropped by thirty percent; in California the MTB phenomenon had exploded. Japan's Shimano was arrogantly invading the market. I—an absolute novice—found myself called on to fight against all this. It was not an easy period. I made many errors because of my lack of experience, so much that early in the nineties there were those who told me I should just forget it."

But Valentino's pride won out. "Ours was not just any company, it was a family company, the company

bearing my name! It was a world-famous brand, so I couldn't just throw in the towel."

In truth, even during those terrible 1980s, Valentino could boast (which he would never do, it not being his style) of having won practically everything. Between 1984 and 1990, Campagnolo won 6 world championships, 5 Giros d'Italia, 6 Tours de France. The outstanding example of this golden period was the great French champion Bernard Hinault, who had associated his name with Campagnolo since the mid-1970s, when he raced for Gitane. In 1985, wearing the jersey of La Vie Claire and using components built in Vicenza, Hinault won both the Giro and the Tour.

Another great champion held the Campagnolo name high during those years. This was the Irishman

Stephen Roche, who was wearing the Carrera jersey in 1987 when he achieved a Triple Crown with overall victories in the Giro, Tour, and World Cycling Championship. Today Roche owns and runs a hotel on France's Côte d'Azur and organizes training camps for cyclists on the Spanish island of Majorca. His students pedal bikes signed by Roche that are equipped with Record or Chorus components by Campagnolo and brakes by the same maker. The year before Roche's exploits, for the first time in history an American, Greg LeMond, won the Tour de France—and Campagnolo was on his bicycles. Today LeMond puts his name on a $4,000 bike that is a rolling advertisement for "Made in Italy": Cinelli handlebar; San Marco saddle; and chain, brakes, gears, and wheels by Campagnolo.

In those same years, two Italian racers became world champions, Moreno Argentin in 1986 and Maurizio Fondriest in 1988. Argentin's Bianchi was equipped with the Campagnolo Record groupset and also had pedals with leather toe clips by Campagnolo; Fondriest, who won on a Legnano also equipped with Record, is currently a bicycle maker and specifies Campagnolo products.

But even these repeated successes, these extraordinary testimonials, did not seem enough to guarantee the future of Campagnolo. Valentino put together a new team and thought up new strategies. And his pride led him to launch new challenges.

C Record Century and C Record

In 2001, the hundredth anniversary of Tullio's birth was remembered with the release of the Record Century, followed by the C Record.

Delta brakes

Campagnolo dominates the high end. The Super Record groupset became the unquestioned standard for high-end bikes, and anyone in the market for a racing bicycle could not help but be drawn to this series of components.

Even so, bicycle components made by Shimano were beginning to show up on the Italian and international market, and Campagnolo had to launch something new, highly evolved, and easily recognizable because of its design. After the celebratory groupset for the fiftieth anniversary, it was time for the C-Record series. It was also now that seven-speed systems arrived. But from the mechanical point of view, the sensational novelty was the Delta brakes.

Campagnolo abandoned the classical caliper design in favor of a completely new mechanism. The body of the brake is triangular (like the Greek letter delta) and contains a complex system of deformable rhomboid levers operated by a cable. When the fingers of the cyclist operate the brake lever, the inner levers are

flattened and expand outward, activating two rocker arms to which, in the lower part, are fixed the brake shoes with their pads. The levers multiply the force applied to the wheel rims, but it was necessary to work out a special, softer compound for the rubber pads on the brake shoes in order to obtain the necessary efficiency in braking.

The braking system was ingenious and physically beautiful, but it turned out to be problematic. The brakes worked too abruptly with braking force that risked causing dangerously sudden stops. Also, the special compound used in the pads proved unreliable when the brakes were applied for an extended period: it was used up rapidly through overheating. When the brakes went from the professional racers who had tested them (and who are used to braking in small, sharp squeezes to keep any overheating of the rims to a minimum) to ordinary cyclists, the problem of the unusual consumption of the pads made itself immediately known. To resolve the problem, the Delta model was temporarily withdrawn from the market to be reintroduced with changes made to the size of the internal levers and to the compound used in the brake pads.

Although not highly valued by the public (because of their weight), Delta brakes remain an outstanding example of technological and aesthetic research.

The evolution of brakes

Old and new compared. In the first version (A) the system is simpler than in the second version (B). Between the two solutions there had been the interim of the Cobalto brakes (C), which repeat the geometry of the Super Record brakes. The final solution (D) is slightly larger than the first version. Also new are the brake pads, made using a different compound.

A
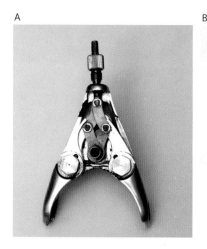

B

C

D
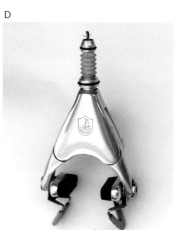

1984

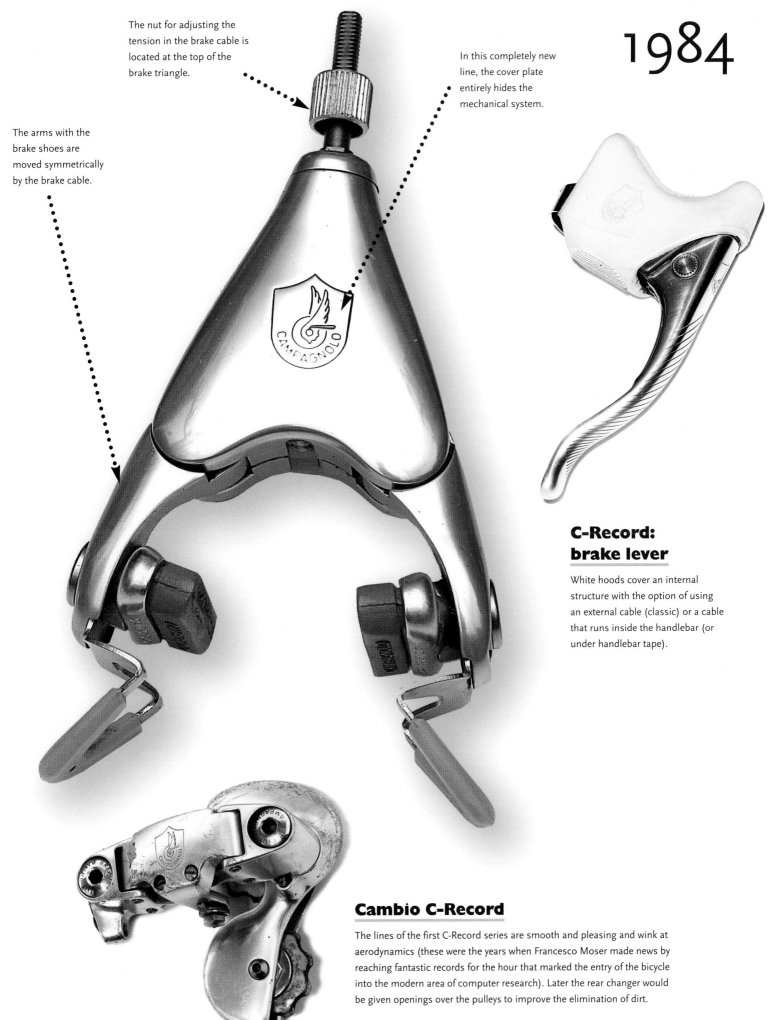

The nut for adjusting the tension in the brake cable is located at the top of the brake triangle.

In this completely new line, the cover plate entirely hides the mechanical system.

The arms with the brake shoes are moved symmetrically by the brake cable.

C-Record: brake lever

White hoods cover an internal structure with the option of using an external cable (classic) or a cable that runs inside the handlebar (or under handlebar tape).

Cambio C-Record

The lines of the first C-Record series are smooth and pleasing and wink at aerodynamics (these were the years when Francesco Moser made news by reaching fantastic records for the hour that marked the entry of the bicycle into the modern area of computer research). Later the rear changer would be given openings over the pulleys to improve the elimination of dirt.

95

The wheels of fortune

Back in 1986, Valentino Campagnolo decided to extend the range of Campagnolo's products to wheels, and thus was born the Ghibli, the first lenticular wheel. Early in the 1990s he astonished the world with the first high-profile wheel, the Shamal, created to meet the need of reducing aerodynamic resistance. In 1994, using Shamal wheels, Miguel Indurain and Eugeni Berzin won, respectively, the Tour de France and the Giro d'Italia. And many were amazed that Berzin used these wheels not only in time trials but also in the mountain stages.

In 1998, the Unità Materiali Compositi ("Composite Materials Unit") was created inside the company with the role of studying new ways of working with alternative materials and alloys, and the development of innovative projects. Only one year later, 1999, saw the intro-

Wheels

Lightness, strength, aerodynamics: These are the characteristics of Campagnolo wheels, fruit of a mixture of technological expertise in the field of composite materials and experience in assembly following the strictest construction standards.

duction of the first Ergopower combination shifter and brake lever made in carbon fiber, and in 2000 came the first two ten-speed *gruppos*, the Record and the Chorus, which returned the brand to a leadership position.

"We work with great tenacity, prudence, and in pursuit of results, paying attention most of all to quality," says Valentino. "Unlike other companies, Campagnolo sees workers and big thinkers as equals. For example, when we started out with carbon fiber, we formed a work group with six people. Today it has 300."

This acceleration of effort led to concrete results. In 1999, company earnings were 125 billion lire. In the fiscal year 2003–05, Campagnolo reached record earnings of 88 million euros, with exports accounting for 72 percent,

The Pirate is light

Marco Pantani testimonial in a 1998 ad for Campagnolo superlight wheels.

a success later further confirmed when the company was awarded the "Compasso d'Oro" award for the Veloce groupset, the Ergopower integrated controls, and the Shamal high-profile wheels.

Toward the end of the 1990s, Campagnolo's standing was increased by further great successes in the Tour de France. There were the outstanding achievements of Marco Pantani, the first Italian racer since Coppi to win both the Giro and the Tour in the same year, 1998. The legendary Pirate raced with the Record groupset and Shamal wheels.

Wheels, from the 1990s all the way to today, have proven to be a new and winning product for the Campagnolo brand. The company's historical construction skills combined with its know-how accumulated in the

sphere of composite materials have resulted in a series of products of unquestioned excellence: from the low-profile Hyperon, the first full-carbon wheels made in Italy with rims and hubs in carbon fiber; to the Neutron, also low-profile, ideal for long and difficult ascents or in complicated courses marked by continuous and repeated changes of speed; to the range of medium and high profile wheels, the Shamal and Eurus, Zonda and Scirocco, Khamsin and Bora models; up to the legendary Ghibli lenticular rear wheel, the preferred choice for time trials. To emphasize that this entire range of products is the result of in-depth research into the science of aerodynamics, all the models have been given the names of prevailing Continental and African winds.

High- and middle-profile

The taller the rim, the more it aerodynamic it becomes. It is also strong and ideal for time trials; with carbon it becomes light enough for ascents. Medium and low profiles make for absolute lightness—just what is needed for uphill racers.

Shamal wheels

The year 1992 was marked by the arrival of the futuristic Shamal wheels. With the Shamal, Campagnolo established the concept of the complete wheel in which every component—hub, spokes, rims—is especially constructed to work together with the others and is thus optimized for that specific model. The Shamal wheels have high-profile rims. Their more than 40 mm of aluminum shine in the sun and make the new wheels unmistakable in photographs and on television. The advantage to the racer is notable: the rims slice through the air and their carrying capacity makes them absolutely stable from the dynamic point of view, even though they are fitted with only sixteen flat-profile spokes. In later versions the number of spokes was reduced to 12. And the spokes, with straight-pull heads, can be drawn to very high tensions, almost double those of a traditional wheel fitted with curved-head spokes. This too contributes to the overall rigidity of the structure.

Another innovation is the way the nipples are hidden inside the rim. The spokes can no longer be operated with a classic spoke wrench but require a 5.5 millimeter socket wrench that can be inserted after removing the tire. The solution seems less than practical, but in reality a wheel with this structure loses shape far less easily than a model with a low-profile rim—yet another reason racers cannot do without these wheels.

The new wheels were made in versions for tubular and also for clincher tires since they were rapidly becoming more popular in cycling. The wheels came packaged with an extension for the air valve. Campagnolo's technical expertise and aesthetic creativity were rewarded when the company was given the Compasso d'Oro for the Shamal wheels and the Veloce groupset.

Rims with aerodynamic lines. The thickness does not exceed four millimeters.

1992

This version of the Shamal wheels is from the last series and has only 12 spokes.

The cassette hub

The adoption of the freewheel unit integrated in the cassette hub, here in the 9-speed version, made it possible to optimize the distance between the sprockets and the spokes. The sprockets were inserted on the cassette and held in place by a lockring. The rear hub is asymmetrical, in spacing as well as flange height, a design made to optimize the centering of the wheel.

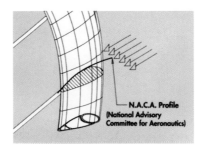

N.A.C.A. Profile
(National Advisory
Committee for Aeronautics)

High-profile rims

The high profile of the rim was based on research done on curves by the National Advisory Committee for Aeronautics (N.A.C.A.) carried out in wind tunnels to study the best profile in terms of aerodynamic penetration.

Facing today's realities and tomorrow's challenges

The world of 21st-century cycling seems light years away not only from its origins but from the way things were barely 30 to 40 years ago. Every sector of the sport has been affected by the headlong rush of new developments, from training techniques to dietary concerns, from pharmacology to technology. Track racing has diminished in importance, replaced by the new specialty of cross-country racing. Certain contests of the past have disappeared, but in their place are new events held in countries that, following a trend already followed in automobile and motorcycle racing, do not necessarily have a cycling tradition but that present themselves as new and attractive markets.

Alongside legendary artisan makers of bicycles are builders that apply innovative techniques. A finished bicycle no longer rolls out of a workshop smelling of grease and hand-worked metal; instead, it's assembled from elements fabricated in shops and plants far distant from one another, perhaps even in different areas of the world. Races have become faster, winning has become more difficult, and today, far more than yesterday, technology plays a decisive role in a champion's success. A series of variables—climate, type of race, length—determines which components the racer opts to use, even the type of bicycle. In this field, as in many others, the effect of globalization has been seen, although the word is often abused and applied blindly to the changes that have occurred in the industry since the end of the 1990s.

Performing successfully in a context involving so much technology is quite difficult and complicated. For this reason, Valentino Campagnolo must be given credit for the enormous skill he displayed in leading the company out of difficult years. Today Valentino is still a prudent man who, like all wise men, has his doubts and his reservations but no longer looks on the future of his family's company with anything like fear. "I believe in the future and invest in the future and accept the challenge," he says. Meaning that even after bringing the brand to the height of fame there are still challenges to be met. Such challenges will always be met with the caution and care that are the guarantee of quality. There are already three such challenges that will affect the present and near future of the company: the sector of clothes, the return of the off-road bike, and the electronic gear changer.

Campagnolo Sportswear came into being in 2003. This branch of the company oversees the design, production, and distribution of technical clothing for road cycling and off-road cycling. In this sector, too, tradition and the most highly advanced innovations go arm in arm. Thus traditional styling is combined with the comfort and performance provided by the application of the newest fabrics.

Fulcrum Wheels dates to 2004. This division

High tech and classic

Campagnolo's entry into the cycling clothing field represents a double value, combining the performance of highly advanced materials with the powerful significance of the company's tradition.

PASSION 2
WEAR

Campagnolo
CYCLING APPAREL

The electronic future

Electronic shifting systems are on the horizon. Following severe tests in the toughest races, the technology has become utterly reliable. Electronics promise immediate and precise gear changes, under any load or condition. Is the market ready? The manufacturers have no doubt: as soon as the public samples the advantages . . .

originally completed the work with high-performance wheels in the road bicycles sector. Three consecutive world road-racing titles with Tom Boonen and Paolo Bettini were convincing proof of the project's value, and in 2007 Fulcrums were extended to mountain bikes, after three years of work spent deciding whether or not go into that sector, which during the 1980s had been the source of so many disappointments that the decision was made in 1992 to abandon it. The official presentations in March 2004 at the International Taipei Cycle Show were followed by dramatic successes, as indicated by the repeated victories of the French racer Julien Absalon, many times world champion from 2004 to 2007 and current Olympic champion.

In 2007, a branch office of Fulcrum was opened in France. Today, the many blogs that constitute a true Campagnolo online community throughout the world are expressing excitement for the expected appearance of a Campagnolo Fulcrum derailleur for off-road bikes.

But the true challenge is the electronic gear changers, the gears of tomorrow.

"We've been testing one for years," Valentino Campagnolo said at the end of 2007. "At the Tour, the Vuelta, and the Giro, and in the great classics. We put it on the bikes of various professionals and then ask them their opinions and suggestions, just like my father did with Magni and Coppi. It is a highly delicate system, and we'll put it on production bikes only when we're sure it will give excellent results. A racing bicycle is not a car. A bicycle is open, the gears are exposed to the sun and rain, the snow and mud and dust. The product has reached a good stage of development. I know that Shimano is working on it too, and maybe they'll get on the market before we do, but the components are vulnerable and I'd prefer to get there perhaps later but with a perfect performing product."

Shimano against Campagnolo, Record groupset against Dura-Ace, Chorus or Centaur against Ultegra.

Julien Absalon

For several years, French racer Julien Absalon, born in 1980, has dominated cross-country racing. Since 2007 he has been a member of the Spanish Orbea team, which uses the leading model of the Fulcrum Off-Road line, the Red Metal Zero Disc Fulcrum. After five months of testing out the Fulcrum wheels, Absalon said, "I'm pleasantly surprised. It is already amazing that in its first year Fulcrum is at the same level as the wheels that I used in 2006, but what I find incredible is how superior they are in terms of response and direction. They have really done a great job!"

The competition continues, first Tullio versus Shozaburo, today Valentino versus Toshizo, president of the Japanese company, one of Shimano's three sons. Meanwhile a third competitor has appeared on the horizon, the American SRAM of Chicago, Illinois. Born in 1987, and most of all a producer of components for mountain bikes, since 2006 it has been making three ten-speed groupsets for racing bicycles.

"With Shimano there is esteem and mutual respect," says Valentino Campagnolo. "They have come here, and we've gone to visit them in Japan. They work in terms of big numbers even while cultivating the ideal of the best. We instead are a metallurgical and mechanical company that works only on racing bicycles. Which is another reason I say you cannot compare our earnings and production figures with theirs."

A metallurgical and mechanical company: Valentino's definition of Campagnolo may seem overly simplistic, even a bit playful. Campagnolo is in fact an immense

rolling laboratory that will not release a product until it has been thoroughly tested—and then tested again. And the people doing this maniacal testing of products years before they are put on the market fall into two groups, amateurs from around Vicenza and the most confirmed champions. The amateurs who are the first to use Campagnolo components are asked to keep what they know to themselves, and there has never been a leak of the industrial secrets they are privy to. The amateurs are too proud of their work to give away secrets, and there is also the matter of their solidarity with a brand that is directly related to their home.

Then come the champions who act as trusted testers. Today Paolo Bettini and Damiano Cunego, Danilo Di Luca and Tom Boonen, along with off-roader Julien Absalon, are among the active racers who test out new materials. Only four days before the world championship at Salzburg, Bettini tried the Ultra-Torque crankset, the system that unites in a single component crankarm and bottom bracket. He

found it perfect, lighter, with less friction in rotation; it provided optimal transmission of the energy applied to the crankset. He got used to it in a few hours and promptly won the rainbow jersey.

"Today," Valentino Campagnolo states with pride, "aside from the plant in Vicenza we have four branches here in the Veneto, and another we set up in 2005 at Pitesti in Romania. There we began with a big shed that soon proved insufficient for the assembly work it had been made to serve; today is it a true plant, and another will open soon in another nearby country."

Nearly 700 people are employed by the production units in Vicenza, Arcugnano, and Pitesti. Campagnolo is also present in more than 30 cities by way of nine agencies and five branch offices: Campagnolo North America Inc., Campagnolo Iberica S.l., Campagnolo France Eurl, Campagnolo Deutschland GmbH, and Campagnolo Japan Ltd. The opening of the last-named office was particularly important: the Vicenza brand, aware of its power,

Di Luca on the wall

Danilo Di Luca climbs a "wall" at the Flèche Wallonne in 2007; his Bianchi is equipped with high-profile Campagnolo Bora wheels.

Ergopower in carbon

Carbon took giant steps ahead. After carbon frames, components were next to be made of carbon, and the market began to understand that the limits of this composite are far from having been discovered. Carbon was initially embraced in cycling with great enthusiasm, but there were then certain negative experiences that resulted from inexperienced manufacturers who put frames on the market that were hardly reliable.

Others, however, paid far greater attention to what they were doing. Campagnolo was among them and brought out a project destined for excellence.

As early as 1998, Ergopower levers had been the subject of a radical change in shape. This reworking was not merely aesthetic but also functional. The distance between the levers and the handlebar was reduced to improve the grip of cyclists with smaller hands. Lever number 2, the one that operated the derailleur, was redesigned to overlap the handlebar during braking. The upper part of the lever body was rounded.

A return spring was inserted in the right lever that served to improve the functioning of the derailleur, much as had been done with the left shifter in 1997. In 1999, the levers were colored black. From then on top models of the company's product range were made in carbon fiber, both the external lever and the internal, which controls the tension in the cable of the front and rear derailleurs.

The carbon used was a fiber with 90-degree braid. The model of the group was printed in white above the lever. The precision and performance of the system was tested and proven, and those who selected Campagnolo knew they were using a system designed for racers that offered a definitive confirmation of every gear change. The Ergopower system also allowed the user to change through several gears with a single action. In this intelligent feature, Campagnolo still leaves its competitors behind.

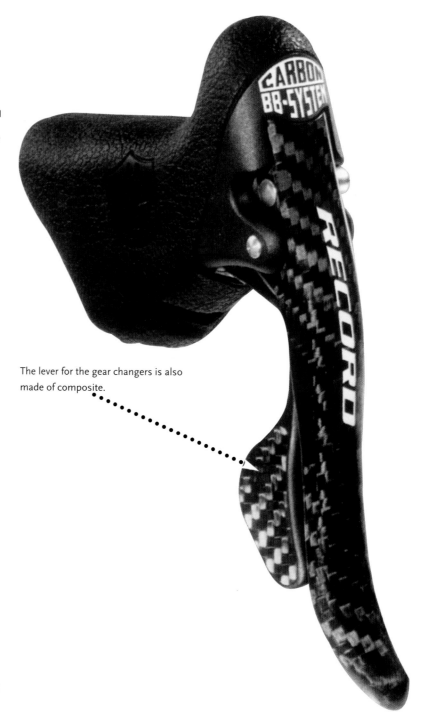

The lever for the gear changers is also made of composite.

1999

From now on, black is the color for Ergopower Record.
The shape of this lever was destined to last for a long time.

Ergopower 1992

In 1992, when Shimano had already presented its STI shifters integrated in the bodies of the brake levers, Campagnolo launched its Ergopower system, a name that ever since has been a focal point for fans of the Italian brand.

The Campagnolo system employs a second lever located behind the brake lever and a button set in the body. The look is elegant, with no cables extending from the shifters or brakes; instead, the cables are internal and routed beneath the handlebar tape. The Campagnolo mechanism makes it possible to move the chain across several gears, in upshifts and downshifts, with a single action of the command lever.

The line

A clean and essential line: the first Ergopower controls looked like this, free of all exterior cables. A blessing for purists and lovers of clean lines on bicycles. In this first version, the brake lever had gone back to being perfectly smooth.

The grip

The Ergopower controls make it possible to shift through several gears with one lever push, both in upshifts and downshifts.

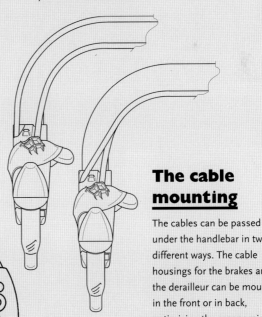

The cable mounting

The cables can be passed under the handlebar in two different ways. The cable housings for the brakes and the derailleur can be mounted in the front or in back, optimizing the ergonomics of the handlebar according to the preference of the cyclist.

Bettini wears Campagnolo and Fulcrum

The bicycle of the world champion Paolo Bettini, a Specialized, "dressed" in Campagnolo: Record *gruppo* and Fulcrum Racing Speed wheels.

FULCRUM.

Pozzato of Vicenza

Pippo Pozzato in the shadow of Big Ben during the prologue time trial of the 2007 Tour de France, which began in London. His Cannondale is equipped with Fulcrum wheels (lenticular on the rear).

has set itself up in the homeland of Shimano. In March 2004 there was the official inauguration of the offices on the twelfth floor of a skyscraper in Yokohama. This has involved the investment of 3 million yen and now has three employees under the general manager Yoji Takeichi. Prior to the establishment of the new office, Campagnolo products had been available in Japan through local distributors. The opening of the branch office was nothing more than a response to increasing demand from a market in which the sport of cycling is quite small when compared to the popularity of other sports. But even in Japan people have discovered that the Campagnolo name means the highest quality and the most refined design.

Today the range of products is very varied: cranksets, shifters, derailleurs, integrated headsets, seat posts, water-bottle holders, low-, medium-, and high-profile wheels, and clothing. It is highly significant that many of today's professional cycling teams entrust their bicycles almost totally to Campagnolo components. As one

example: the Cannondale SuperSix of Filippo Pozzato, Vicenza racer for Liquigas, mounts shifters, front and rear derailleurs, cassette, chain, brakes, and seat post made by Campagnolo, along with Fulcrum wheels. There are also numbers that give an immediate sense of the standing Campagnolo enjoys in the world of professional cycling: in the 2008 racing season, seven Pro-Tour teams (including QuickStep-Innergetic of world champion Paolo Bettini) and nine Continental teams used Campagnolo components on the bikes of their racers. In 2007 Campagnolo was world champion three times: at Stuttgart, with Paolo Bettini, in the individual men's road race and with Marta Bastianelli in the women's; and with Julien Absalon, in the mountain bike championship.

The distinguishing traits of Campagnolo products have remained the same and today are further amplified: responsiveness, lightness, strength, reliability, beauty. In unison, they create the history and the prestige that no competitor can equal.

The 10 speed

Two thousand was the year of the change. Campagnolo took everyone off guard at the Salone del Ciclo in Milan, saluting the arrival of the new millennium with the presentation of a completely revolutionary groupset. After the debut of carbon, the Vicenza company landed a knockout punch on its competition by presenting the first ten-speed groupsets.

Working on increasingly reduced thicknesses and tolerances, Campagnolo had managed to insert another gear in the cassette, drawing the attention of technicians and fans. The reduction in thicknesses made it possible to use wheels designed for 9-speed systems (9V) without problems, but it did require, naturally, the application of a new chain, called the C10. Also presented was a cassette with a maximum cog of 29, a wink at lovers of great mountain slopes that also meant a valid alternative to the use of a triple chainwheel (which for the time being was reserved to nine-speed groupsets). And the weight? Even here Campagnolo managed to amaze: the increase in weight of the tenth sprocket was compensated for by a complete redesign of the groupset. All told the 10-speed group (10V) weighs less than its nine-speed predecessor.

Credit for this goes to the use of new materials. This was the first time that a bicycle derailleur was presented with a front cage made of carbon fiber braided at 90 degrees. With the use of parts in titanium, the front changer alone made for a savings of 39 grams over the preceding version.

The rear derailleur was also available in a version with a medium cage necessary to support the sprocket maximum of 29 teeth.

Ten speeds were also applied to the second groupset in the Campagnolo line. Those who wanted a 10V power train could also choose the Chorus groupset, although in that case the gear changer remained in aluminum. Even so, the Chorus component was lighter than the 9V version by 34 grams.

The cassette

One . . . two . . . three . . . yes, there are ten. It may have seemed impossible to put so many gears on one cassette, but Campagnolo beat its competition in the race. Shown in the photo is an even more special cassette since it has a final sprocket of 29 teeth. An effective range with fewer gears would have been very difficult.

Ergo Brain

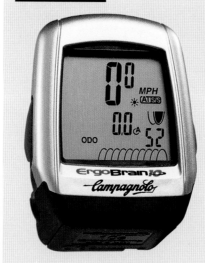

The Campagnolo bicycle computer made its debut in 2000. It is integrated with the components since the buttons to control it are fitted directly into the brake hoods, and the system is able to display the gearing by means of an instantaneous measurement of speed and pedal cadence. The Ergo Brain made its debut in the 9V version but became common in the 10-speed version.

2000

Perma Link

The C10 chain has an especially narrow width to match the new measurements of the cassette. A special link was used to connect its ends, called Perma Link, which can be installed only by using a special kind of parallel pliers.

Titanium screws contribute to holding down the weight: in total 39 grams less than the 9V version.

The external cage in carbon fiber distinguishes the Record changer.

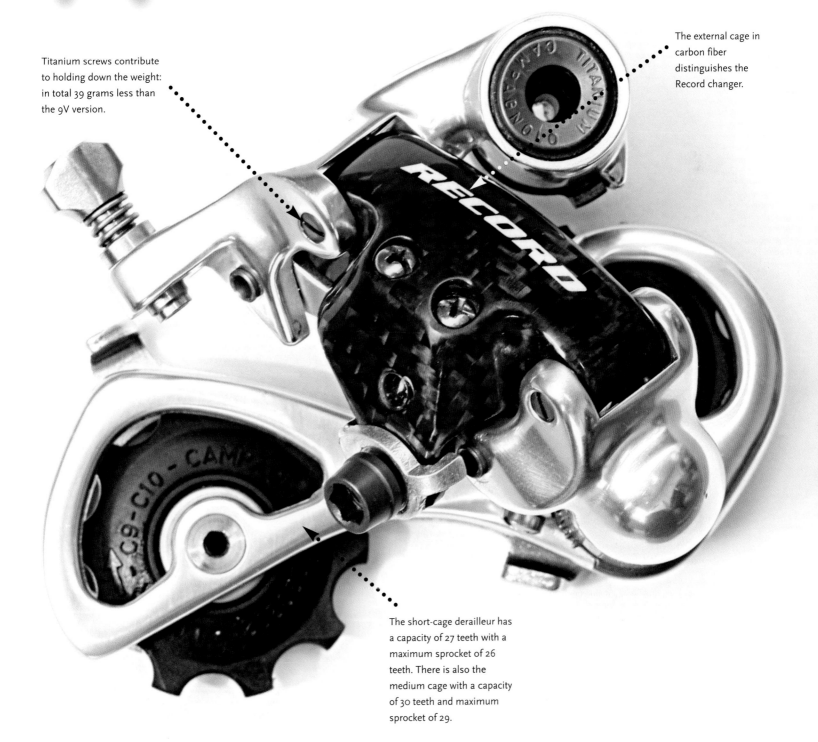

The short-cage derailleur has a capacity of 27 teeth with a maximum sprocket of 26 teeth. There is also the medium cage with a capacity of 30 teeth and maximum sprocket of 29.

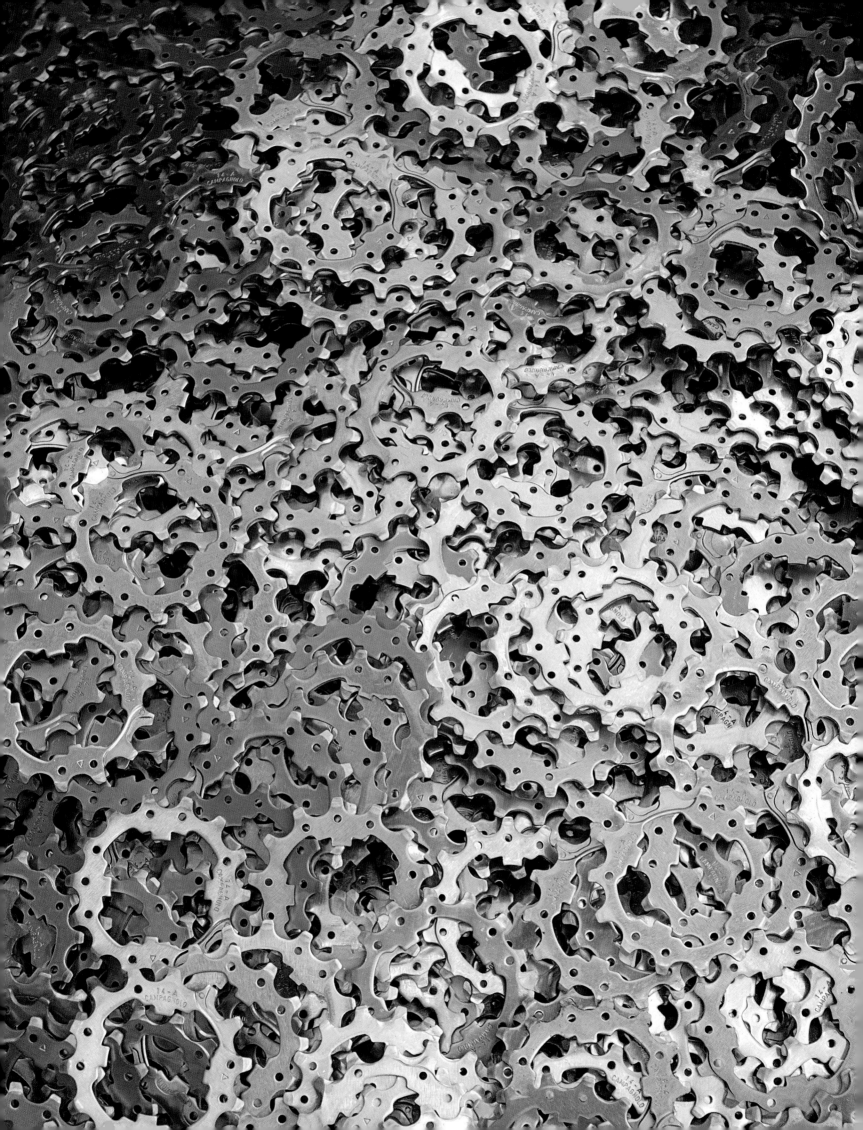

Inside the Factory

An idea and its measurements: R&D

From design to product: prototypes

The Test unit

The rulers of carbon

The factory is Campagnolo's home. From the earliest days in the back room workshop of Tullio's father's hardware store, to the workshop in Porta Padova, and finally to the plant on Via della Chimica, the factory, the place where things get done, has been—along with the roads and velodromes—one of the two great driving hearts of the company history of Campagnolo.

An idea and its measurements: R&D

In his time, and in his own way, Tullio Campagnolo performed research and development. Continuous work on improving designs, the search for better technological performance, for materials of greater reliability, the maniacal attention to detail and to suggestions from the people actually turning bicycle pedals, and finally the ability to translate studies and inventiveness into products that can be manufactured on an industrial scale—all this, thanks to the example set by the company's founder, still constitutes the Campagnolo identity. Today, notebooks and direct contact with Coppi or Merckx—perhaps seated at a table in a restaurant—have given way to a design sector with the highest technological profile, with structural calculations made by computer, three-dimensional computer-aided design (CAD) images, and an internal testing department in which special simulation machines reproduce the stresses from the road in the laboratory.

Giuseppe Dal Prà is in charge of Campagnolo's department of Research & Development. He has been with Campagnolo since July 1975: "I joined the company as an engineering draftsman in the engineering office. There were six of us, three working on the product, three on processes of industrialization. We were still in the plant in Porta Padova, in the middle of the 'age of Tullio.' And I can truly say that everything or just about everything has changed over those thirty years and more of work. The ways of thinking, the methods and deadlines, the materials—aside from the competition, the market. But it's true: R&D, research and development, is part of Campagnolo's genetic code."

Today, Dal Prà, born in Vicenza, oversees a group of 19 people involved in design. "We usually work in groups of three or four on specific projects: gears, brakes, cranksets . . . This is the creative phase: around this table we have to put together market demands—

The design table

The engineer Giuseppe Dal Prà (center) with his R&D team at a design table.

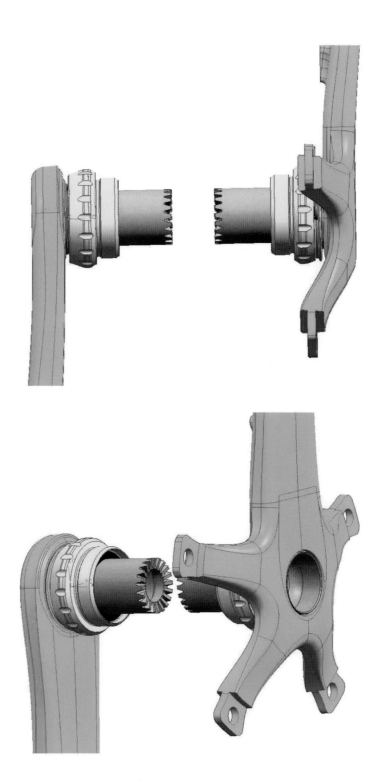

Everything in a small space

Ultra Torque moves the connection between the crankarms to inside the bottom bracket. There is thus less external obstruction, with more space for the rider's ankles.

CAD to the fore

Computer aided design (CAD) has revolutionized the design and analysis process, speeding the translation of ideas into prototypes.

115

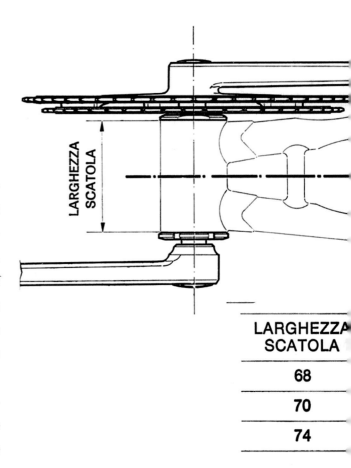

LARGHEZZA SCATOLA
68
70
74

the ones that make us come up with new lines of products year by year—with engineering ideas that result from our internal know-how. It's also the time for risking, taking a gamble, maybe even playing around a little. Of course what counts is maintaining a clear vision of the objective, most of all in terms of time requirements and the feasibility of the idea. An idea is great when the measurements work out, when it can be translated into industrial production."

Coordinating the production chain is of fundamental importance: product design and development. "We work in teams. And even if ninety percent of the time the original idea comes from the project head, its creation depends on the level of sharing the objective."

Over the last decades, the changes in thinking and in production methods have caused changes in expertise. "In the past, experience counted more than anything else, practical experience," Dal Prà observes. "Armed with empirical wisdom, you could move ahead on the basis of trial and error. We can no longer do that. The deadlines for design and production have become increasingly tyrannical: it is essential to get to the market at the right time. And the prototype must be as close as possible to the final version, the one that will go into production. Fortunately, we have the assistance of information and enormously powerful instruments: the CAD, for example, makes it possible to visualize a project as a structural whole, to simulate the three dimensionality of the project with great precision, and to calculate its dimensions down to the tiniest fractions, absolute and relative. Being able to use these instruments has necessarily led to an elevation and a specialization of the technical knowledge needed by anyone working in the design sector. It makes sense that the area of design, along with those of testing and composite materials,

has been among the areas in which the company has made its greatest investments of personnel: this is the technological heart of Campagnolo. This is where the patrimony of internal knowledge that is the company fortune is hidden and cared for."

Over the span of his thirty years with the company, Dal Prà has experienced many ups and downs, times of difficulty and times of important revival. Two particular periods of company history stand out in his mind.

"The first was during the second half of the eighties," he recalls. "For Campagnolo, it was a time of crisis. Shimano had introduced index shifting, and we were having a hard time keeping up. It was a decisive moment: we looked each other in the face, went through a process of self-criticism, and then radically rethought our design methods. Thanks to the design and production of rear hubs with freewheels with cassettes and sprockets that until then we had made only for racing teams, we finally managed to create an index system that was competitive. But more than anything else it took a change in our mental approach, with a strong investment that brought

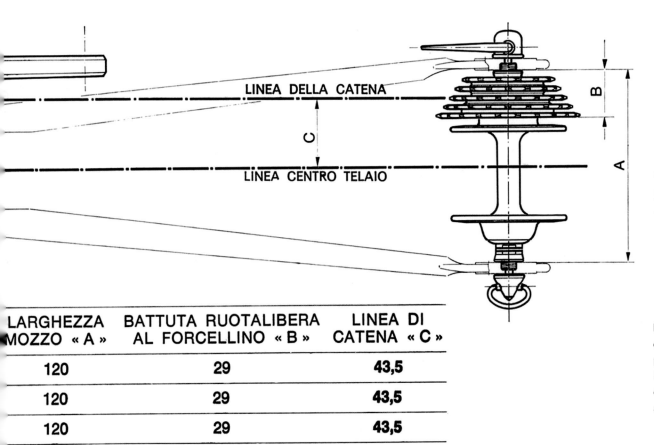

LINEA DELLA CATENA

LINEA CENTRO TELAIO

LARGHEZZA MOZZO « A »	BATTUTA RUOTALIBERA AL FORCELLINO « B »	LINEA DI CATENA « C »
120	29	43,5
120	29	43,5
120	29	43,5

Measure for measure

This drawing, taken from catalog no. 18, represents the chainline with the relative measurements for the centerlines of the crankset and hub and the width of the freewheel cluster. Alignment between the sprockets and the chainrings is essential for precise gear changes. Framebuilders and component suppliers have always worked together.

out knowledge and experience."

Another great milestone in the relaunching of Campagnolo came in the second half of the nineties, when the company foresaw the strategic importance of composite materials.

"The search for lightness combined with strength has always been a fundamental objective, even when we worked on metals and alloys," Dal Prà says. "The thermal treatments, the hardening, improved the strength and life of materials, but the arrival of carbon was a true revolution. We too began making parts in carbon: seat stays, the spacer in the bottom bracket, then the Ergopower control levers, and finally the cranksets, which today are one of the most beautiful Campagnolo objects, even in the aesthetic sense. But what distinguished Campagnolo in terms of its use of composite materials is having known how to acquire this technology by transforming it into an industrial resource. Even today, production in carbon requires a great deal of manual skills, an artisan activity in knowing how to wrap the layers of carbon one on top of the next to form the

structure. It is an extremely costly method if you don't have access to low-cost labor, such as that of the Far East. Campagnolo, with an enormous investment, was able to industrialize the production procedure, assuring, in the repeatability of the pieces, excellent quality standards that usually are not easily achievable in large-scale production."

Quality and excellence translated in industrial terms: this is the Campagnolo alchemy, as Dal Prà attests. "Campagnolo, because of its tradition, is and always will be forced to hold the high-end market. That means making certain its products perform better than those of the competition, which can count on being competitive in terms of market prices. And quality and excellence require continuous efforts at innovation: you have to keep raising the bar a little higher, you have to keep making the challenge. That is our future."

Carbon crankset

New technologies were on the attack. The use of carbon fiber in cycling reached a notable maturity with more and more components being made in composite.

Two thousand two was the year of the new Record crankset in carbon fiber. This very interesting novelty did not fail to awaken admiration and amazement, but there was also a certain amount of skepticism. However, the Vicenza company was well aware it could not risk false steps and had adopted solutions drawn from the most technologically advanced sectors. Indeed, the new crankset was derived directly from the aerospace industry and promised rigidity, strength, and absolute reliability. Unfortunately, the price was high, and this, at least in the beginning, seemed to be the primary limit to the spread of its adoption.

That same 2002 was also the year of the Hyperon wheel. Campagnolo placed it within the Climb Dynamic range, dedicated to hill-climbing specialists. The low-profile rims in carbon fiber promise lightness suitable for a hill climber: 520 and 710 grams are the numbers recorded, respectively, for the rear and front wheels. The rims used on the rear have an asymmetrical shape that partly compensates for the difference in spoke angle caused by the presence of the cassette. The hubs, too, are made in fiber, called HPW Carbon. The body is in composite of a differentiated thickness, while the right flange of the rear wheel is still in alloy (that being the freewheel side, where the spokes have greater tension).

The triple crankset with a dedicated derailleur made its debut among the 10-speed systems, and the Cambio Record was enriched with a version with a longer cage able to support sprockets with up to 29 teeth, impossible to handle with the classic short cage.

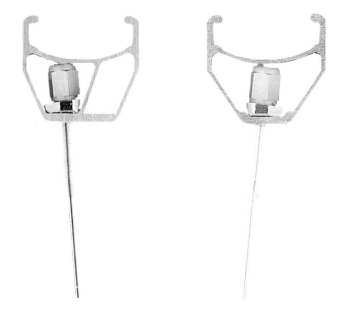

Asymmetrical rims

The rear and front rims are different. The rear is asymmetrical to permit a better mounting of the spokes and to respond to the demands of the offset of the rear wheel, or dish, caused by the presence of the cassette.

Carbon hub

The carbon hubs are made with differentiated widths. Although very strong, they are not overly heavy, contributing to a pair of wheels that weigh only 1,230 grams.

The Record design is distinguished, also in this version, by the integration of the fifth arm in the crankset.

2002

High-pressure carbon fibers ensure absolute rigidity. The shape is wider and squarer than in the aluminum version.

There is complete compatibility with all the 10-speed components already on the market.

Hyperon wheels

Decidedly light with rims and hubs in carbon fiber: they tip the scales at 1,230 grams.

119

From design to product: prototypes

A robot for molds

A robot-controlled machine works on a mold for a prototype of the Ergopower brake hoods.

"I came to Campagnolo in 1973, with the five-speed changers. And I was asking myself: what's left to invent? Thirty-five years have gone by, and we've never stopping making new things, always new . . ." This is Gianni Borga, head of the Prototype department, the mechanical heart of Campagnolo. It is the place where new ideas are made, where designs become reality, in fact where they often conflict with reality before becoming objects on their way to becoming mass-produced products. This is where prototypes are made.

"We're the company's designers; every year we make Campagnolo's prêt-à-porter, we construct the models that make the season. Also for us, a lot of things have changed over the last thirty years. In the beginning we did everything by hand, beginning with the designs. Now the designers, using CAD, work in three dimensions, and it is like already seeing the object in its physical reality. Even so, I can state with certainty that we are the heirs of Tullio's file. This is where the creativity of the project meets the manual reality of its transformation into an object and the engineering reality of its mass production. We are the crucial test of a project's value."

Borga oversees seven people in his department, which is the pride of Campagnolo's mechanical knowhow. They work at full speed, almost without interruption, and under great pressure. The introduction of testing machines revolutionized the way of working, making it safer and faster, while also causing a vertiginous acceleration of execution times. "Years ago it took more than one season to make a complete groupset; today, we do more than one in a year. You can say that our department never closes. But despite the pressure, we are buoyed by being such a crucial part of the company. In the twenty years that I've been here, I don't remember anyone ever quitting or changing work."

What is a prototype? "You could say it is the embryo of a product. It is the first stage: it arises from the plan and can be made of a variety of materials. Aluminum, steel, plastic materials, etc. For working composite materials we provide the mold of the prototype, and the same thing applies to plastic or rubber. The prototypes in metal we create ourselves, from a cast. Every material has a different set of tools and requires a different approach, but the fundamental thing is the work in symbiosis with the designers. As far as a design or a project is well conceived, it is at the prototype stage that its viability is determined. Our products are often assemblies of different parts: and here comes the moment of truth. The tolerance of measurements must be calculated to

The prototype team

The prototype department is a crucial area of the factory. Its work schedule is intense, but it approaches each task with extraordinary team spirit.

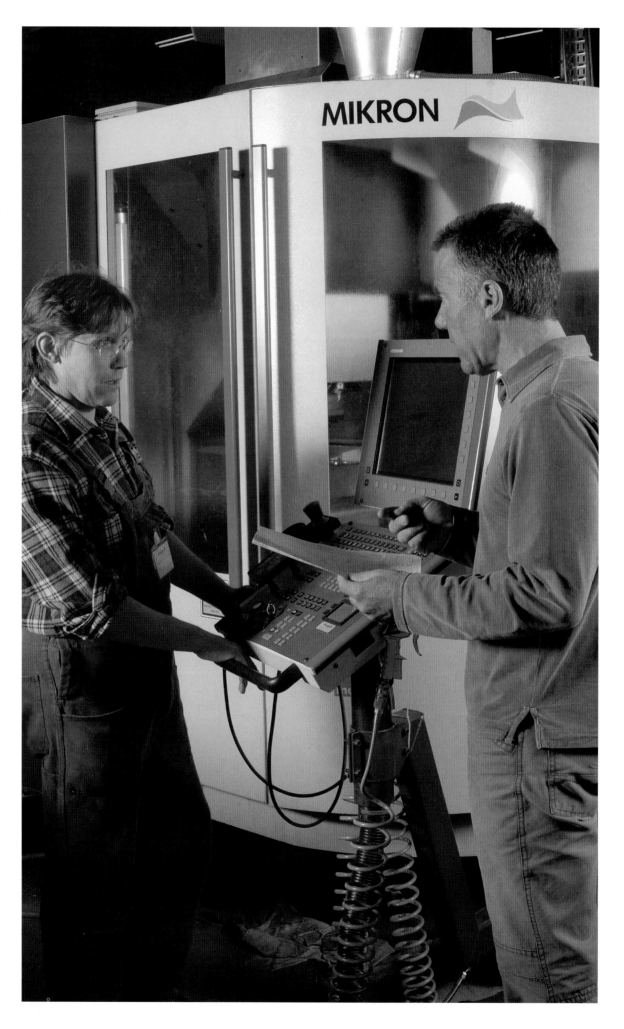

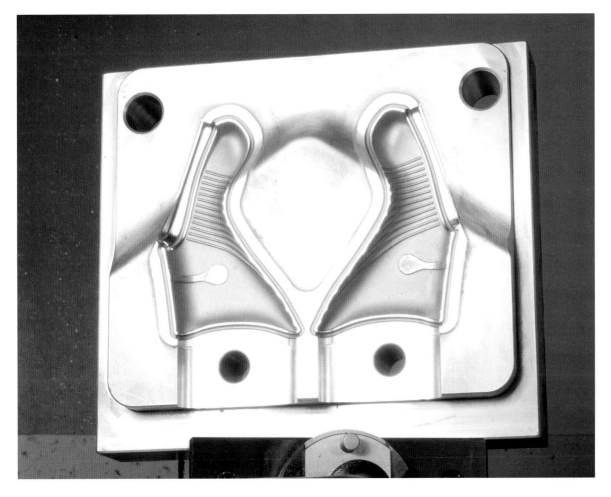

A brake hood

Every mold, like every prototype, is produced in the prototype department. Here is another look at the Ergopower rubber hood mold.

the micron. Something may well seem theoretically impossible, but we have the support of experience, practical knowledge. Which is nothing you can get from a manual or some theoretical examination. You build it up day by day, year by year, working on the actual piece.

"Here, we can say that almost all our professional training is still internal: our ways of working are a patrimony that we want to preserve, handing down the knowledge among colleagues of different generations. And that too contributes to our group spirit, even when faced with difficulties, with the stress of increasingly urgent demands, for more performance. I always say that people have to walk to us. Physically walk. It would have been ideal if the Prototype department had been

located near the stairs leading to the first floor where there are the designers. Because a prototype comes into being from both the idea of the designer and the hands of the technician.

"Once the prototype has been made, a pre-series of 5 to 10 pieces is produced. These are sent to the Testing and Approval unit. And there another group effort begins. The information collected by the testers and inspectors is sent back to us, so we can make modifications and adaptations to the prototypes until we get the model will make it through the tests and go into production."

Fulcrum

In 2004 Campagnolo introduced a new brand: Fulcrum. A new logo and new identifying color (red) established the identity of special wheels strongly based on the technology used by the Vicenza company.

The Fulcrum wheels greatly pleased the public, which was initially a little perplexed by the new brand. The wheels met with approval because of their strength and performance, but the true change happened when they began to be used by professional racers (and immediately by teams in the forefront of the international peloton). The compatibility of the cassette was also offered to those not using Campagnolo components, opening the market to bikes with Shimano cassettes and derailleurs.

A few years later, when Campagnolo returned to take on the mountain-bike sector, it was with Fulcrum. It had already done so, directly with the Campagnolo brand, in 1989, presenting the Centaur groupset (a name later used in the racing sector) and the Euclid groupset. The two groupsets were distinguished by their large assortment of components. The Centaur boasted three types of shifters, three derailleurs, and three brake levers. For all intents and purposes, there was no off-road situation for which one would not find the optimal solution.

The wheels presented in 2007 for mountain bikes represented a new

challenge that was highly appreciated by fans. The debut with sponsorship for world champion Julien Absalon says a lot about Campagnolo's plans for the market—so much so that Fulcrum did not stop at wheels. The debut of Ultra Torque cranksets (for the road sector) in 2007 represented a further step that many hope will take the form of more work dedicated to off-road cycling.

External bearings

An Ultra Torque crankset also for Fulcrum. This introduction is dedicated to the "non-Shimano" groupsets.

2004

Medium thickness rims: the strength of the new wheels begins here. The braking tracks are machined.

The flange of the rear hub is different to permit improved balance of the wheel.

The spokes are aerodynamic and of differing thicknesses to reduce the formation of eddies that slow air movement.

MTB from Campagnolo

The Euclid groupset. Together with the Centaur of 1989, it marked the short appearance of Campagnolo in the mountain-bike sector.

Optimized tension

Straight-headed spokes are used. This permits an optimal tension along the full length of the spokes.

The Test unit

There is no Campagnolo product that does not pass through (more than once) the Test unit. Through the windows of the enclosing boxes, you can see the testing machines connected to computer monitors that reveal the results of tests performed on every component: shifters, cranksets, brakes, wheels, chains, everything.

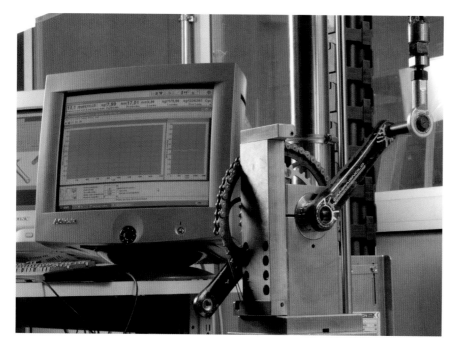

Computerized strength testing

Every component is tested following protocols that usually exceed the measurements prescribed by international testing rules. The information collected by way of software is filed in a database. The page opposite shows a Fulcrum crankarm under test, with a motorcycle chain employed to support greater tension than a bicycle chain could resist.

This testing is an essential element to Campagnolo since the key to the company's success is the quality of its products, their reliability, efficiency of performance, safety, and long life.

The young engineer Valentino Franch belongs to the most recent generation of Campagnolo employees. He arrived four years ago, and for the past two has been in charge of testing of product development. "Our contribution of data acquisition, the critical elaboration of data, and the generation of *a posteriori* analyses, has three distinct phases of application," Franch says. "Two are closely related to the procedures of product development. When the input for the elaboration of a new

component comes from marketing and from the design area of R&D, the Test unit gets to work analyzing whatever competition is on the market. The reference products are instrumented, meaning fitted with instruments for reading data: a kind of black box that collects and makes available the information that is desired on performance efficiency, strength of materials, and whatever else is desired, in the form of structural calculations, which are given to the designer to work out a computer-designed virtual prototype. While this is happening, the testing unit is preparing and setting up the methodologies of testing and the instrumentations that will be applied to the prototype when it is transformed from its virtual form to something physical, ready to be tested."

The test is performed by machines—most of them designed and produced by Campagnolo itself—that reproduce in the laboratory the stresses of road use. Every product is subjected to stress tests to evaluate aspects of performance, strength, and safety, gradually compiling a picture that is used to adjust the prototype and, most of all, that makes possible its engineering, which improves its characteristics and identifies the best solutions for its future phase of industrial production.

But once validated and put on the market, a product makes periodic returns to the testers. This is the third distinct phase referred to by Franch. "After a product has been declared ready for the market, we're called on to verify its maintenance of the standards of quality and safety. In order to do so, according to a set schedule we monitor each product to see if it is maintaining the levels of efficiency we set for it when it was released, seeking in that way to head off uncontrolled changes."

The Testing area represents the present of the company and probably also its future. It is a relatively recent investment that has transformed what was originally

instinct and experience and was expressed in complex evaluation lists, into a patrimony of data collected and elaborated by computer, easily accessible and available of integration. "Also in this field, the professional level of the person in charge of testing is extraordinarily specialized," Franch observes. "Instrumenting the bikes, collecting and elaborating the data, and setting up the tests are carried out by engineers, who are often also the creators or at least provide the inspiration for the great machines built to test the products and the software that elaborated the data. All the same, it requires great teamwork: even the technician performing the most routine chore, one dictated by protocol, has the sensitivity to pick up a datum, a variable that the machine communicates, making his contribution essential to our success."

There are tribological tests, those that deal with the friction and wear of surfaces in motion and in contact, and there are other tests performed in special laboratories. A physical-chemical laboratory, equipped with electronic microscopes, measures and analyzes all the non-metallic components: plastics, fibropolymers, carbon fibers, ceramics, mixtures for brake shoes. Another laboratory tests the strength and efficiency of surface coverings for metals. There is also a metrology laboratory involved in the verification and validation of the exact geometry of the parts of components.

Even so, the test of actual road use has not lost its importance. Just as Tullio followed his champions in order to directly hear their impressions of the performance of his products, Campagnolo still gives fundamental importance to reports from users in the field. The opinion of a champion, like that of an everyday cyclist, is put in relation to data collected by instruments mounted on the bicycle. "For cars and motorcycles, it is easier to attach data-collection instruments, but for a bicycle it

Paolo Bettini and the Ultra Torque

As often happens in the world of cars, the best testers are not necessarily famous racers. Even so, today, as in the period of Coppi and Merckx, there is nothing like a great victory to consecrate the quality and success of a product. "A few weeks before the world championship in 2007, Paolo Bettini was intrigued by the Ultra Torque, the crankset system with an integrated bottom bracket and spindle, which after more than a year of laboratory tests and six months of field tests, we had supplied to Danilo Di Luca," says R&D manager Giuseppe Dal Prà. "The Ultra Torque is an enormously fascinating component, even simply in terms of aesthetics; I can't rule out that the world champion was merely attracted to its appearance. The fact is that Bettini asked to try it in practice and was immediately won over by its rigidity, the ease of weight transfer when pedaling. He put it on his bike, took it to the world championships, and won. For the Ultra Torque there could not have been a better baptism."

is not easy to install instruments—that are as delicate as they are precise and sophisticated—on narrow structural supports like a frame or fork," says Franch. "There is then the question of relative weight: these tests for collecting information are done more often than not during practice, since it's unlikely that a rider will agree to carry the added weight of one or two kilograms in a race. With a telemetric system every action made—a gear change, a braking, pressure on the crankarm—is transmitted to a center of data collection installed on the following car; thus one can see live the information and compare it with the impression of the tester."

Opposite
Black box

To collect the data necessary to evaluate a component's overall performance, bicycles are fitted with recording instruments, including a central black box that receives inputs from all over the bicycle.

The rulers of carbon

There is one area of the Campagnolo factory that is strictly off limits to all visitors, and even to most employees. This is the Composite Materials Area where all the parts made of carbon are produced. Numerically, it is a very important department, since more than about 130 people work there. It was set up at the end of the 1990s with the foresight that composites would become the new frontier of bicycle components. "A big investment also in terms of personnel," says the engineer Gabriele Ciavatta, director of the unit, "because the working of carbon fibers requires a high level of manual labor, from preparing the molds to applying the laminations. But unlike what happened in many other areas of cycling production, Campagnolo decided to industrialize these processes, to render their quality and performance level stable and not susceptible to the variables of handwork operations."

Carbon made a powerful entry in the production

Woven fibers

Carbon fibers are arranged in a weave of black filaments similar to those of straw chairs. This type of fabric (called "skin" in industrial slang) is arranged in layers inside a mold that will give form to a lever, a hub, a crankarm, and so on. The direction of the "skin" reflects the specific mechanical characteristics of the carbon structure.

Junctures

In the past, differences in the electric charges of carbon and aluminum created a galvanic current, a migration of electrons between the two materials that eventually caused problems at junctures. Today the cohesion of physically different elements is assured by the evolution of adhesives, as is the case with the carbon crankarm and the aluminum chainring of the Record groupset.

cycles of the bicycle industry because of its characteristics of light weight, strength and durability. Treated with special epoxy resins, carbon fibers provide resistance to the effects of time superior to that offered by metals.

"Campagnolo uses a variety of technologies in the working of carbon, from hand layering to high-pressure molding to rubber or foam expansion; from rolling on mandrels of layers of carbon fibers to using a stamping press. We began with the production of wheel rims, then came crankarms, hubs,

water-bottle holders, seat stays, and then derailleur and Ergopower shifter components. In the Ergopower model, the brake levers are made of carbon, as are a series of other minor products, such as spacers and the caps for headsets."

Working carbon requires great skill, and Campagnolo decided to bring home the know-how and protect it jealously. "Carbon fiber is a very expensive raw material, and its use without the rigor of engineering, which seeks to optimize manufacturing procedures and keep waste to a minimum, would be, as has often happened, a great risk for a businessman," says Ciavatta. "This led to the institution of strict procedures for the handling of the product from its arrival as a raw material at the company to be transformed into a product. It is worked in specially clean rooms, maintained at constant temperatures and humidity, and it is protected from dust and all other potential pollutants. Every transfer of material, from storing it in envelopes to its working and refining, is monitored and recorded to have every step under control and prevent malfunctions in the production chain. Control of the parameters is very important. A cycle of production that uses carbon fibers is an irreversible process; if something does not work, it all has to be thrown away, and such waste must be prevented. The lay-up of fibers, or lamination, is checked, the weight, the coating cycle. An ultrasound test checks the structural integrity of the product when the work is finished."

The data collected during the production cycle are put into a computer system: parameters of the process, percentage of waste, monitoring of the quality of the work. All this to provide useful statistics and to standardize as far as possible the product as well as to identify as needs that must be dealt with technologically or that require changes in the training of technicians.

"The strength of our work unit is revealed in how it managed to stabilize and strengthen a production process involving materials that are as precious as they are delicate," says Ciavatta. "And in finding how to best integrate carbon with the rest of the components made of different materials. In that sense, the science of adhesives is essential, for it makes it possible for components of different natures to exist side by side in a single product."

Hub section

The Composite Materials Unit, with more than 130 employees, produces all of Campagnolo's carbon components. Carbon parts require a high level of manual labor in the preparation of molds and the application of laminations and surface finishes.

Worldwide Campy

The cult

Passion & fetish

Three quarters
of a century

To the world, Campagnolo is more than just a quality brand name in the sphere of racing bicycle components. Thousands of collectors of cycling memorabilia, from Europe to North America to Asia, look upon objects bearing the Campagnolo emblem with a kind of visceral worship.

The cult

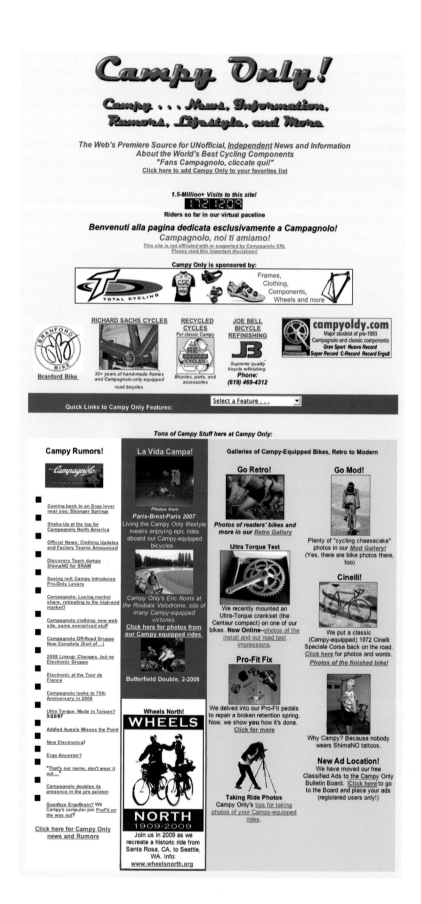

A few years ago, the *Wall Street Journal* listed Campagnolo among the world's best-known brands of sporting goods. The truth of this is reflected in the fact that there are so many fake Campagnolo items in circulation today, just as there are knockoff versions of the most prestigious brands, such as Rolex, Gucci, Louis Vuitton. Not so long ago an Austrian cycling tourist wrote the Vicenza office complaining about a Campagnolo groupset he had bought on eBay that had turned out to be defective. The company had him send the pieces and then analyzed them closely: they were out-and-out fakes.

In December 2004, the authoritative American magazine *Bicycling* published a long article about the "Campy-Mania" spreading across every continent. Written by Mark Riedy and entitled "The Cult," the article analyzed the phenomenon with well-reasoned argumentation worthy of a professor of sociology. The basic axiom is that Campagnolo, far from being merely a company and a brand name, is instead a cult, a creed professed by millions of faithful followers. By way of proof, Riedy presented six key points. The first of these confers on the founder, Tullio Campagnolo, the dimension of a prophet, a sort of St. Paul. Instead of seeing the light on the road to Damascus, Tullio got his enlightenment on the twisting curves of Croce d'Aune and went on to invent the device that marked the beginning of the modern technological revolution in cycling. The second point: to its disciples Campagnolo is an act of faith about which there can be no question, not even when a Campagnolo product simply does not stand comparison with that of a competitor. True believers are always ready to overlook the less brilliant periods and the near misses in the company's long history. Third point: the glory of Campagnolo is celebrated by its saints, meaning the legendary champions that have served as its standard bearers, from Coppi to Merckx, from Hinault to Pantani.

This "sacred iconography" plays a decisive role in the construction of a mechanism of identification-emulation that serves the faithful. Point four: Campagnolo is addictive. Anyone doubting this need only take a glance at the number of ads for Campagnolo items on eBay. There may well be more ads for Shimano products, but those come with "zero poetry" attached. The Campagnolo pieces have more appeal because of their history, which makes them desirable even when no longer usable on a new bicycle. They possess value because they emanate the fascination of tradition. Fifth point: The Campagnolo fan is a maniac who sees Shimano as his enemy, an enemy that stands for everything that is the opposite of what Campagnolo stands for. It is as though Shimano lacked the spirit of heroism, theatricality, passion, innovation, and tradition that is instead the quintessence of Campagnolo. Which then brings us to the sixth and last, which is a tautology:

137

International Campagnolo

The Czech national team posing in front of the entrance to the Campagnolo factory in Porta Padova, during the early 1970s. Below, the Campagnolo-equipped national team of China, in Tiananmen Square early in the 1980s.

"Only a bicycle fitted with Campagnolo is a bicycle fitted with Campagnolo."

Riedy moved easily from the sacred to the profane to reach the point where he could define Campagnolo components as "lovely, curvaceous, sexy." And, he claimed, the bicycles that "wear" them are the "the most seductive in the world." There are those who have similar ideas concerning Campagnolo and have gone so far as to have the company logo tattooed on their body. Exaggerations of the passionate, hyperboles of fanatics. Perhaps. The fact is that ranks of admirers along with collectors of memorabilia have a visceral veneration for the name Campagnolo. Such fans are easiest to find in the United States, but they show up in unexpected locations, such as the Arab Emirates, Russia, and also Japan, homeland of Shimano.

More than enthusiastic collectors, these are in many cases truly rabid fans, for their passion is not directed only at their idol but is also aimed against anyone who attempts to chip away at the myth. In 1995, Eric Norris of Davis, California, inaugurated the website Campyonly.com, a treasure trove of information on Campagnolo that is often the starting place for somewhat humorous slogans, most of them directed at that perfidious competitor, Shimano. Two examples: "Just say ShimaNo" and the totally nonsensical "Shimano Causes Brain Damage."

Ultra Torque

The time has come to assign to history the square bottom bracket spindle. The revolution in the shape of the bottom bracket had begun several years earlier, and various fantastic and functional solutions had already appeared on the market. Putting bearings outside the bottom bracket and the use of an oversized spindle offer structural rigidity without precedent. The evolution of the bottom bracket toward greater rigidity has moved toward connections designed to increase the size of the surfaces in contact.

The project that Campagnolo presented in 2006, foreseen for the market in 2007, was called Ultra Torque. It is not a simple through axle since, in fact, there is no single axle. Mounted on the left and right crankarms are semiaxles that form a single body with the crankarm. The two parts of the axle are joined in the middle of the bottom bracket shell by means of a Hirth joint, a special toothed shape already used in mechanics because of the great loads it can support.

The system found favor and was embraced by the public but also by mechanics, since its assembly is truly simple. Having installed the exterior caps, one must only insert the two parts and connect them using the central bolt. All that is needed is an Allen wrench to complete the operation, and one can begin pedaling without further adjustments.

Compared to the earlier system, no change is made in the value of the Q factor (the distance between the external planes of the crankarms), but compared to other systems of through axles, the awkwardness of the exterior parts has been reduced. Since the cranks and the semiaxles form a single unit, the dimensions are optimized. The savings of 100 grams, on average, of the new Ultra Torque system make it possible to lighten the entire range of components that adopt this solution: this means practically the entire Campagnolo line with the exception of the base group, Xenon. This

Skeleton brakes

The brakes Campagnolo introduced in 2006 are called Skeleton brakes. The lattice structure is made by forging (to align the crystal structure of the alloy) and offers greater strength along with less weight than the preceding system.

group, however, was brought up to ten speeds, thus marking the final movement of Campagnolo to ten speeds throughout its range.

2006

Record crankset

Ultra Hollow monocoque technology for the crankset: the arms of the crankset are molded to create a hollow structure. The reduction in weight is equal to the gain in strength.

Ultra Torque technical diagram

This is the CAD-designed diagram of the Ultra Torque system (in particular the central bolt of the connection). Today all components are made with absolute precision in their dimensions to achieve optimized performance in every situation.

The teeth of the Hirth joint are the heart of the new system. Once the two semiaxles have been assembled, the solidity is absolute.

Passion & fetish

Wearing Campagnolo

Fans manage to wear Campagnolo even away from their bikes, as is the case with the belt buckle on the page opposite; others make Campagnolo a kind of second skin.

GIANNI BRERA
IL GIGANTE E LA LIMA

Unfindable

In 1993, on the tenth anniversary of the death of Tullio Campagnolo, the company printed a biography by Gianni Brera, *The Giant and the File*. Since it was not made for distribution in the usual book channels, the book soon became a highly sought collectable. It was one of the last works by the great sportswriter, who died in a car accident in December 1992.

All this enthusiasm makes for an extraordinary market. Lickbike, a company in Oak Park, Illinois, sells all the Campagnolo products imaginable and possible, roughly 187, such as a Record Pista crankset for around $300; a 2006 Chorus double front derailleur for $93; a Record steel/titanium 10-speed cassette for $250; Campagnolo ball bearings for $8; 1972 chromed/alloy pedals for $10; a Campagnolo keyring, $20; a racing wheel bag, $28; a poster of Miguel Indurain, winner of the Giro d'Italia 1992 riding his Pinarello bike, $18; Shamal Ultra Clincher Road wheels, $1,088; or a Big corkscrew, $189.

Early in 2008, more than 400 Campagnolo items were being auctioned off on eBay, part of an ongoing rush taking place on a planetwide scale to buy up anything bearing the famous name, whether new or used. Among the items being hotly contested by visitors to online auctions were seat posts and cranksets, pedals and bottom brackets, hubs and 10-speed cassettes, brakes and brake levers, and of course individual tools and complete toolkits. Among the most sought after pieces were two Neutron Ultra wheels, contested by 17 fans. The opening price was 20 euros; they were sold for 251. A total of 27 potential buyers were vying for a Campagnolo Record Compact 170: in the end it was won by a German from Nuremberg for 221 euros. Also on the auction block were various curiosities, among them a Campagnolo jersey for children, which sold for 7 euros, a Campagnolo alloy rim for Alfa Romeo, snatched up for 12 euros, and an old hand derailleur (81 euros). There was also a bronze luxury-model Big corkscrew (110 euros).

Rare ads (such as that of 1975 with Eddy Merckx, Clay Regazzoni, and Walter Villa advertising together

the many-faceted genius of Campagnolo), photos, vintage posters, such as those of various winners of the Tour (LeMond, Indurain, Riis, Pantani), and other memorabilia can be found at auction on eBay, but also on internet sites selling "antiques" or in such larger stores as Amazon.com. There are then certain truly rare pieces, destined to be seen in photographs or only by the intimate friends of their legitimate owners. Such as, for example, the series of three ceramic plates depicting birds and signed in person by Campagnolo that he gave as gifts to his distributors on the occasion of the New York Bike Show of 1980. No one today remembers why the birds were chosen, unless Commendator Tullio wanted to imply that his products could fly.

Highly sought after and, by now, unfindable, is the biography of Campagnolo written by Gianni Brera in 1993, *The Giant and the File*.

One beautiful object eagerly sought by many collectors is the limited-edition set of three different silver-

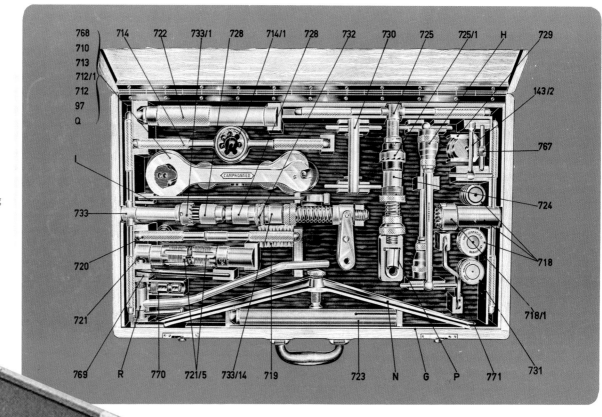

The tool chest of miracles

From catalog no. 15, a drawing of the complete Campagnolo tool kit, shown below in an ad from 1983.

Colors of the rainbow

An old Campagnolo pullover, emblazoned with the rainbow colors of the world championship. The Campagnolo brand is highly sought in vintage clothing.

gilt belt buckles produced in 1981 and presented in a special case. This special article was made on the occasion of the eightieth birthday of Tullio Campagnolo; the first buckle is round and bears the classical "winged" logo; the second is rectangular and reproduces an historical photo of the young Tullio as a cyclist at Croce d'Aune; the third is oval and bears the "Prodotti Campagnolo Speciali" logo.

Another rare piece highly sought by collectors is the special box with the 9 pieces of the Record groupset, made by Campagnolo in 1983 for the company's fiftieth anniversary. More than 10,000 of these were made, each with a numbered certificate of guarantee. There are about 200 examples of these cases around, and the price of each is about $10,000 in the United States and 6,000 euros in Europe.

Of particular attraction to collectors are items bearing the company's trademark, which changed over time

and was produced in a variety of versions. These compose a collection of about 200 versions, from the first of 1953, and related to them are company pins. Highly sought after are the three pins made for the 1984 Los Angeles Olympic Games in which the Campagnolo brand was distinguished by being the official and exclusive provider of technical assistance in the cycle races.

Corkscrews and nutcrackers

Tullio Campagnolo expressed his creative abilities in a variety of fields. His genius was often aroused by moments of even minor irritation when he found himself unable to do something and wanted to find a way to make the execution of that thing more simple. So it was with the famous Campagnolo corkscrews, which appeared in 1966 following Tullio's encounter with an especially difficult cork. Until then even the finest bottle of wine had to be uncorked using brute force, grasping it between the knees, inserting a screw attached to a handle in the cork, and then pulling on it with as much force as was needed. After injuring a hand in this very operation, Tullio decided the procedure had to be simplified. In a few minutes he designed what today is the most widespread corkscrew in the world, the one with the self-centering bell that is positioned over the cork with a tempered steel screw that is wound into the cork and then lifted upward by means of side wings, making it possible to open a bottle even using only one hand.

So proud was Tullio of this corkscrew that he made it his symbol and gave it away as gifts or prizes at the many events in which he participated.

Today the Campagnolo Corkscrew is highly desired by collectors throughout the world, most of all the "Big," a 29 cm long glazed version. It was taken off the market in 2003, but in response to enormous popular demand was brought back in 2005. There are versions in 18-carat gold, silver, and bronze.

Less known are another three objects dear to Campagnolo collectors that have nothing whatsoever to do with bicycles: a nutcracker designed to open walnuts of any size without difficulty (Tullio was extremely fond of them), a tennis racket with an aluminum handle, and the Campastria, a device designed to keep pants pressed that proved quite handy to Tullio during his frequent trips.

There are three pins, in gold, red, and blue, each of which presents a different Campagnolo logo surrounded by the Olympic rings.

The company's catalogs, from the first of 1953 to the most recent of 2008, which celebrated the seventy-fifth anniversary, constitute an absolute must-have for the passionate Campagnolo fan. In addition to the historical value there is also the didactic element. Leafing through them one cannot help but note how complicated and detailed each component is, from the smallest and simplest to the largest and most complex.

Three quarters of a century

For Campagnolo, 2008 was a special year since the company, founded in 1933, celebrated its seventy-fifth anniversary. Three quarters of a century borne well. Campagnolo decided to celebrate the anniversary together with its many admirers, a community that thanks to the technological opportunities offered by the Internet has been growing steadily larger. The company website presents an open window on Campagnolo and Campy World. The site seems infinite and is kept up to date with technical information on products as well as services and events related to the brand and the world of bicycle racing. During 2007, the Bora Art Contest was held on the Campagnolo site, in which visitors were asked to create a graphic depiction of the Bora, the high-profile wheel, one of the company's most popular products. A jury reviewed all the submissions and selected ten, and online voting in January 2008 then determined the winner. The top vote-getter was "Blue Wind," by the Brazilian Silva Hudson Malta. The planet-wide dimension of the Campy Cult phenomena was reflected in the fact that, aside from the Brazilian winner, the ten finalists included four Americans, two Britons, a Canadian, a German, and a Dutchman.

Campagnolo's seventy-fifth anniversary

Bora

Silva Hudson Malta, graphic artist from Rio de Janeiro and winner of the Bora Contest, explained his design: "The blue line is the wind, the Bora. I like the way Campagnolo names its wheels after winds! The white line is a team of cyclists moving very fast, with a smoke effect. The power of speed is depicted by a simple white line. The fluttering 75 represents the past years and the future of Campagnolo and the spread of its philosophy to every corner of the world. The transparency of the 75 is an ode to Campagnolo technology, and the numbers were created by waves of carbon. My idea was to show how the Campagnolo years were full of knowledge and technology. The use of an ancient character for the numbers represents tradition."

was also celebrated in the saddle. On June 15, the tenth edition of the Gran Fondo Campagnolo was held, almost 216 km up and down the valleys of the Belluno Dolomites, with the pass of the Croce d'Aune as the final springboard for reaching Feltre, where the marathon begins and ends. In the days immediately after the race, a Passion 2 Ride was held, with technical discussions of theory and practice that involved the presence of experts, including former champions and journalists. Dozens of other events were organized throughout the year in every part of the world by the Mad4Campy community.

The Gran Fondo Campagnolo

This poster is from the fourteenth edition, in 2008.

The monument to the Genius

At least 150 monuments or markers have been set up in honor of cyclists, most often in memory of the excitement they gave their crowds of fans. Fausto Coppi boasts 12 such markers, Marco Pantani now has 10. Some mountains are studded with sculptures of champions, such as the Alpe d'Huez in France, which looks like an open-air art gallery. Certain small towns have acquired fame for having been the birthplace of a racer, and many such locales have returned the favor, such as San Martino di Colle Umberto's monument to Ottavio Bottecchia, the first Italian to win the Tour de France. There are also places that merit a monument because they were the scene of unforgettable events. On the Col de Perjuret in France there is a monument at the curve where Roger Riviere fell into a ravine, ending his promising career. At Ste. Marie de Campan a marker indicates the location of the forge where the legendary Eugene Christophe, having broken his original fork in a fall, made himself a new one under the watchful eyes of Tour officials.

Standing out among this crowd of monuments to famous cyclists are two that refer to people who did much to benefit the sport. The first is to Jacques Goddet, the mythical director of the Tour de France, recalled on Tourmalet.

The second is to Tullio Campagnolo, the bicycle racer who forever changed—and vastly improved—cycling.

The monument to Campagnolo was inaugurated on June 24, 1995, on Croce d'Aune, at the site where the young racer was struck by the "lightning bolt" of the realization that something had to be done. The work presents the story of that day in two parts, one showing Campagnolo busy struggling with the rear wheel, the other showing him coming up with the idea to make the operation easier.

The day after the inauguration of the monument, the first edition of the Gran Fondo Campagnolo was held, it too designed in memory of the great Tullio Campagnolo. Its route—need it be said?—includes the pass at Croce d'Aune.

11-speed Super Record

With the clarity of hindsight, it seems clear that Campagnolo was soon going to release a new version of the Ergopower controls. The shape of the commands had been the subject of a certain amount of criticism, and the market demanded something more ergonomic. Even so, no one expected the new Ergopower controls to have so many new features. So many, in fact, that Ergopower itself no longer seems like the primary feature. What put the controls in shadow was a completely reworked system: 11 speeds. This sensational and unexpected news was accompanied by a name that always brings pleasure in association with Campagnolo: Super Record. Thus the model that had met with such great success during the 1970s and 1980s returned to the fore.

For its 2009 range, presented at the end of 2008, Campagnolo decided to revolutionize its transmission. The electronic system, although nearly ready for production, was put on hold in favor of a transmission with an extra speed. Campagnolo also sought to raise the overall level of all its groupsets (the "Raise the level" concept dominated the 2009 catalog). The Super Record was not intended to replace the highly popular Record. It was placed above it, with formidable characteristics. The gear changer was completely redesigned. The external cage, in carbon, was made far larger to provide for the increased requirements of functional precision caused by the change in available space that resulted from the extra speed. The value of rigidity in the external cage is put at 150 percent. The Ultra Shift design includes new sizes for the teeth leading to further improvements in shifting. The materials were also changed. The new treatments make possible greater rigidity in the gears and increased resistance to corrosion.

The design of the new Ergopower commands includes larger shapes to increase the surface of handrests. The shapes have been optimized to favor grips from different positions in the saddle. Whether the rider is upright or in the more aerodynamic position, the brakes and derailleur can be operated with facility and precision. The shape offers a new grip, available on the upper part of the control. This is an ideal rest for those longer stretches, just as aerodynamic extensions once were, at least for a short time. The 11-speed system will also be applied to the Record and Chorus groupsets.

2009

Ergopower Ultra-Shift: increased handrests

The completely innovative style of the new Ergopower controls includes three openings to lighten the levers of the Super Record. The lever makes it possible to move the chain among three gears in ascent and five in descent.

Details in titanium mean maximum lightness: the gear changer weighs only 172 grams.

The derailleur body is larger to provide absolute precision in functioning.

The cage is extremely light, with an exterior in composite material. It is also very strong thanks to its new size.

Wheels with 11 teeth with ceramic bushings for the upper and ceramic balls for the lower.

New shape for the sprockets

Six sprockets in titanium, five in steel with special treatments; the cassette for the Super Record is an ideal compromise between lightness and strength. The six largest sprockets are mounted in groups of three on two aluminum carriers that give them greater rigidity than the 10V. This is also part of the Ultra Shift technology of the new 11V system.

The Last Mile

Brief history of
the gear changer

Campagnolo instructions
for use: 10 practical
suggestions

The palmarès

A brief panoramic view of how bicycles have changed gears over the last eighty years.
Ten practical suggestions for getting the best out of Campagnolo components.
And finally an overview of forty years of cycling successes signed Campagnolo.

Brief history of the gear changer

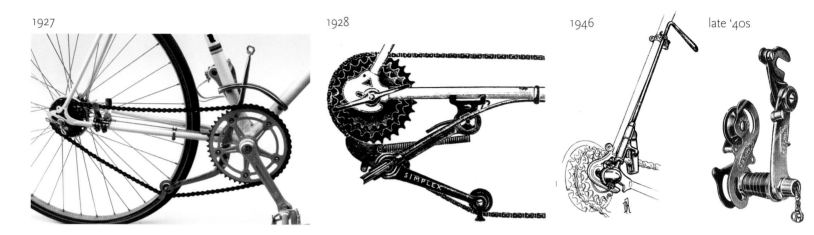

1927   1928   1946   late '40s

Early 20th century

People began thinking about gear changers for bicycles around the end of the 19th century. The need to abandon the single gear became clear with the arrival early in the 20th century of large-scale races, which awakened public interest. In 1910 high mountains were included in the **Tour de France**, leading racers to seek **variable gears** for their bikes. Such changers were initially ignored by race organizers, but within a few years they moved against them, claiming they were unsporting in a race in which the only difference between competitors was supposed to be physical strength. Many racers themselves were hesitant to adopt systems that complicated bicycle mechanisms, adding weight and also increasing the amount of friction.

1920s

Various methods of changing bicycle gears were presented during the 1920s. France was one of the most active countries in this regard. The sport of bicycle touring was increasing in popularity, inspiring much technical research. Around **1927** the Nieddu brothers presented a version that came to be known as the **Vittoria** gear changer. No longer was it necessary to get off the bike to change gears. A backpedal was still required, but the advantages were notable. From France (in **1928**) came

the Simplex gear changer, which made it possible to change gears without the backpedal. This initially had only two gears, and its strength was quite limited. A few years later the **Huret** came on the market, it too characterized by a single pulley located near the freewheel.

1930s–1940s

The idea of the gear changer had taken hold. By then even a front derailleur was increasingly being included. At the beginning of the century there had been a first experiment in this sense, but now the speed of evolution significantly increased. The form of bicycle gear changers, influenced by racers, has always followed a route toward simplicity, lightness, and reliability. For this reason various systems that were apparently highly modern did not enjoy great success when they were first released. **The dual-rod changer** designed by **Campagnolo** soon proved itself worthy in those very terms, also in contrast to the **Vittoria Margherita**, which had been the favorite of many racers. During the second half of the 1940s the Simplex represented an important step in the evolution of the gear changer. Its concept was innovative because it included a chain-guide with a cage (with double pulleys), which directed the chain to the rear sprockets. This was in effect the same system used today on gear changers.

1951 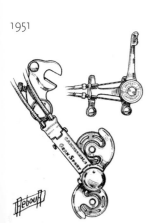 1973  1990  1999 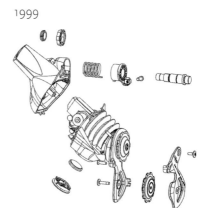 2007

1950s–1970s

The later evolution of the bicycle gear changer included the introduction of the **parallelogram mechanism**. This arrangement made it possible for the chain to move across a greater number of sprockets. The **Campagnolo Gran Sport** immediately proved to be a functional idea. Over the span of about ten years all the manufacturers of gear changers adopted this solution. Even today, mechanical gear changers are fitted with a parallelogram mechanism operated by a cable with a return spring that makes changing gears very rapid.

From then on, most attention was concentrated on the materials, on their **mechanical efficiency** and on the **weight** of components. For many years the standard arrangement included six rear gears and two front (with the exception of three in the front for special situations).

The **Shimano** brand rose to importance in Japan during the 1950s. Within a few decades it was competing with Campagnolo for supremacy in the manufacture of bicycle components. In 1973 Shimano released the **Dura-Ace** groupset in Europe mounted on the bicycles of the racers of the Shimano-Flandria team (that of Freddy Maertens in the world championship of 1973). This division of the market has remained in place although complicated by the arrival of other brands, such as SRAM and FSA.

1980s–1990s

Specialization and the evolution of cycling led to an increase in the number of rear gears. From six the move was made to seven, then eight, nine, and ten speeds. The arrival of **nine speeds** marked the beginning of the introduction of different standards, meaning that Campagnolo products were no longer interchangeable with those of the Shimano series. The adoption of **indexing** in the middle of the 1980s by Shimano and developments in the search for spaces on the freewheel led to differences in thickness of the gears of the two systems, factors that must be kept in mind by bicycle fans and by racers (as when changing wheels in races). The 1990s saw important changes in bicycle transmissions, including the abandonment of control levers on the downtube of the bicycle. The front and rear derailleurs are controlled from the **handlebar** by way of systems **integrated** with the brakes.

The 2000s

With the new millennium the subject was **electronic** gear changers. Two attempts were made by the French **Mavic**, and although these did not have immediate results they made clear that there is a great deal that can be done in the field. At this point, electronic gear changers seem to be the new frontier to explore.

Campagnolo instructions for use: 10 practical suggestions

Not everyone reads the instructions that come with bicycles. Here are several tips and a few tricks to help keep a modern bicycle in shape.

1. The torque wrench

Do people really use it? By now, this tool is considered indispensable in any workshop. Superlight components and the widespread use of carbon fiber have made it indispensable. Campagnolo provides the necessary defined torques in its instruction sheets.

2. No grease on carbon seat posts

Do not apply grease to the shaft of a carbon seat post made by Campagnolo (or by any other manufacturer). If you really want to protect it from infiltrations of water, it is best to use an appropriate friction paste. Grease would make the surfaces slippery, and the result would be that more force would be required to tighten the seat post collar than is recommended by Campagnolo.

3. Grease on threads

It is advisable to grease the threads of the bottom bracket cups and pedals. Greasing the first will avoid irritating creaking while pedaling, the second will make them easier to remove if needed. Nor is it necessary to overtighten the pedals. The opposite threading is designed so that the direction of pedaling tends to screw the axle on the crankarm.

4. Carbon wheels? Special pads

This is an error that even professionals commit. Wheels with braking surfaces in carbon require the use of special pads that will not suffer from the sudden increase in temperature caused by friction on carbon (which does not disperse heat the way aluminum does). Campagnolo has designed pads that initially "dirty" the braking surface, but that render it optimal for use in operation. For this reason, it is not a good idea to repeatedly clean the braking surface: doing so means beginning the break-in process all over again.

5. Maintenance of brake pads

Brake pads should be periodically checked, not only for the extent of wear (according to Campagnolo the wear limit is the bottom of the grooves), but also for alignment since they should meet the wheel rim directly. Bear in mind that the wheel causes a certain bending and thus irregular wear.

6. Cables and housing: crucial zones

Gears and brakes are operated by means of cables that run through special housing. It is important to maintain the housing at the optimal level of functioning to guarantee precision gear changes and the safe operation of the brakes. Campagnolo housings are lined with Teflon to optimize cable movement. There is no reason to grease a housing since doing so would only make it gummy and prevent smooth movement of the cable.

7. Chain, when and how

A worn chain, aside from ruining chainrings and sprockets, is also at risk of breaking. To check the state of a chain, you have to measure the distance between six external links. According to Campagnolo, this distance should be at most 132.6 millimeters. Furthermore, remember that you must use a new retention pin each time you install a Campagnolo chain. Otherwise, the security cannot be guaranteed and there is the risk of serious danger. When installing a chain, follow the manufacturer's instructions to the letter.

8. Perfect cleaning of the chain

Through regular use it is normal for dirt to adhere to the chain. Removing this dirt can be difficult, and using solvents is not a good idea since there is the risk of ruining the exterior treatment of the links put on Campagnolo chains to optimize their functioning. Follow this method: before going out for a ride, put a great deal of lubricant on the chain. As you pedal this lubricant will loosen the encrustations on the links so that when you get home cleaning the chain with a simple wipe of a rag will be greatly facilitated.

9. Attention to the position

Before removing the saddle and seat post, you need to record the current position for putting them back. Otherwise, getting it right again can be annoying. Remember, however, that Campagnolo clearly calls for the use of nothing more than adhesive tape to indicate such positions: never make notches or scratches on components (especially if they are made of a composite material).

10. Do you have small hands?

A trick to get the brake levers closer to the handlebar grip is to insert a small screw in the body of the handrest near the release button of the brake lever. This is an ingenious solution, but it does not have certification from Campagnolo, so anyone who does it is on his own.

The palmarès

Despite the increase in competition over recent decades, Campagnolo has continued to add new successes to its already long list of palmarès. For example, the last world road champions used a Campagnolo gear changer on their bikes. And in the past ten years, the Giro has been won 6 times by Campagnolo men.

Year	World Championships	Giro d'Italia	Tour de France
1968	Adorni (*photo opposite page*)	Merckx	Janssen
1969	—	Gimondi	Merckx
1970	Monseré	Merckx	Merckx
1971	Merckx	G.Petterson	Merckx
1972	M.Basso	Merckx	Merckx
1973	Gimondi	Merckx	Ocaña
1974	Merckx	Merckx	Merckx
1975	Kuiper	Bertoglio	—
1976	Maertens	Gimondi	Van Impe
1977	F.Moser	Pollentier	—
1978	Knetemann	De Muynck	Hinault
1979	Raas	Saronni	Hinault
1980	Hinault	Hinault	Zoetemelk
1981	Maertens	Battaglin	Hinault
1982	Saronni	Hinault	Hinault
1983	—	Saronni	
1984	Criquelion	Moser	Fignon
1985	Zoetemelk	Hinault	Hinault
1986	Argentin	Visentini	LeMond
1987	Roche	Roche	Roche
1988	Fondriest	—	Delgado
1989	—	Fignon	—
1990	Dhaenens	—	LeMond
1991	—	Chioccioli	Indurain
1992	—	Indurain	Indurain
1993	—	Indurain	Indurain
1994	—	Berzin	Indurain
1995	—	—	Indurain
1996	—	—	Riis
1997	—	—	Ullrich
1998	—	Pantani	Pantani
1999	Freire	—	—
2000	Vainsteins	Garzelli	—
2001	—	Simoni	—
2002	—	—	—
2003	Astarloa	Simoni	—
2004	—	Cunego	—
2005	Boonen	—	—
2006	Bettini	—	—
2007	Bettini	Di Luca	

Bibliography

Bartali, Gino. *Tutto sbagliato, tutto da rifare*. Arnoldo Mondadori Editore, 1979.

Bergoglio, Carlo. *Vita misteriosa dei Giri d'Italia*. Editoriale Sportiva Milano, 1946.

Brera, Gianni. *Il Gigante e la Lima*. 1993.

Chany, Pierre. *La fabuleuse histoire du Tour de France*. Editions de la Martinière, 1988.

Conoscere il ciclismo. Rizzoli, 1985.

Marchesini, Daniele. *Bianchi: A Bicycle Alone in the Lead*. Bergamo: Bolis Edizioni, 2007.

Marchesini, Daniele. *L'Italia del Giro d'Italia*. Società Editrice il Mulino. 1996.

Picchi, Sando. *La grande storia illustrata del Giro d'Italia*. Ponte alle Grazie Editori, 1992.

Stagi, Pier Augusto. *Colnago, bicicletta*. Prima Pagina Edizioni, 2007.

Storia della bicicletta. Edizioni del Prado, 2002.

Photographic sources

Archivi Alinari, Florence: 9, 10, 17, 50.

Archivio Bianchi, courtesy F.I.V. E. Bianchi: 89, 105.

Archivio Campagnolo, courtesy Campagnolo: 4, 22, 23, 24, 27, 28, 29, 35, 44, 49, 53, 54, 55, 57, 63, 72, 74, 75, 78, 79, 80 (2), 81, 82, 88, 89, 90, 91, 96, 97, 98 (2), 99, 101, 102, 103, 104, 106, 107, 110, 111, 113, 115 (2), 116, 118 (2), 119 (2), 124, 125 (3), 130, 132, 133, 135, 137, 138, 139 (2), 140, 141 (3), 144 (2), 145, 146, 147, 148, 149 (3), 150, 151, 154.

Archivio Cinelli, courtesy Antonio Colombo, Caleppio di Settala, Milan: 68.

Archivio Marzotto, courtesy Marzotto Press Office, Valdagno, Vicenza: 26.

Bicycle Club Magazine, Tokyo, special edition "All About Campagnolo": 28, 29, 53, 55, 70, 71, 73, 86, 92, 93, 95, 130.

Civica Raccolta delle Stampe Achille Bertarelli, Milan: 8, 9, 10, 14, 15, 19, 20, 36, 37.

Civico Archivio Fotografico, Milan: 14.

Corbis: 56, 62, 79.

Collezione Alberto Masi, courtesy Alberto Masi, Milan: 70.

Collezione Gino Cervi, courtesy Gino Cervi, Milan: 12, 46, 142.

Collezione Paolo Facchinetti, courtesy Paolo Facchinetti, San Lazzaro di Savena, Bologna: 30, 31, 60, 61.

Collezione Paolo Gandolfi, courtesy Paolo Gandolfi, Parma: 2, 9, 16, 18, 21, 59 (2), 65, 83 (3).

Collezione Paolo Rubino, courtesy Paolo Rubino: 28, 29, 38, 39, 63, 73, 86, 87, 94, 95, 100, 101, 110, 111, 145, 152.

Farabolafoto: 40, 71.

Gianalberto Cigolini, Milan: 24, 25, 39, 42, 41, 74, 112, 113, 114, 120, 121, 122, 123, 126, 127, 128, 129, 130.

Mavic, courtesy Mavic Press Office: 84-85, 153.

Olycom: 13, 16, 32, 45, 47, 51, 58, 63, 66, 69, 76, 77, 82, 108, 109, 113, 151, 156.

Photomovie: 63, 67.

From "TuttoCarlin, " an exhibition of the works of Carlo Bergoglio, curated by Gino Peccherino, Ivrea: 40.

Shimano, courtesy Shimano Press Office: 84-85, 153.